CHOOSING PEACE:
MIRACLES ARE DECISIONS

CHOOSING PEACE:
MIRACLES ARE
DECISIONS

&G

REV. SCOTT P. ANSTADT, PhD, DCSW, CAC-2

AND

Deb Byster

And

Consultation with Deb Brown

-ANST

To order additional copies of this book, contact:
Xlibris Corporation
1-888-7-XLIBRIS
www.Xlibris.com
Orders@Xlibris.com

Contents

Dedication

This book shares with all folks whom we have met and have yet to meet the joy and peace gained through truly listening to God's ever-present inspirations.

My thanks go to dear loved ones, especially Deb Brown, who encouraged us on and inspired us with mirror reflections of light and love.

PREFACE

If anything would convince me it is time to write this book, it was the circumstances the Holy Spirit showed me to do so. Two years before I wrote this book, I went through several life changes. My life changed in every way imaginable. It seemed everything was left up in the air. Each day when I awoke, I felt a sense of dread and panic. Consciously I was thinking of doom and self-resignation. Perhaps this was my inner self saying to me, 'There is a better way to see my life". That is when prayer became my morning ritual, more than at any other time in my life up to that point. My daily prayers were always answered as I look back on things, but I was not always aware of this absolute fact. My faith was not as yet strong enough to open my eyes and ears and truly see the Lord's work. I was still trying in my small way to make sense out of things that were happening.

One day, I sent an e-mail to someone who had posted to a spiritual Internet board. Her reply had energy of so much comfort that I was able in that brief Holy Instant to feel my attunement with the great universal mind of God. Her response was friendly, but the energy beneath the words was a message of comfort like I had not felt in years. I knew again that no matter what changes I was undergoing in my earthly affairs, God was guiding me, and there was nothing to fear. Well, as events unfolded, this woman became my soul mate and wife.

Shortly thereafter, she found a bulletin from a seminary I had sent for some time ago. Rather than put it aside, I was surprised at the small voice inside me saying, "The time is Now". I called the next day and was accepted with special consideration because my inquiry was past the deadline. That was the beginning of my ministerial studies. About a year later, after studying at the heart level within the seminary program, I heard a voice within saying again "the time is Now, write the book".

For several days, I attempted to convince myself that I was not ready and besides, I didn't know what to write. Yet, it was too late. That still voice of the Holy Spirit was all too familiar to me now. In a Holy Instant my mind flipped to a solid and knowing awareness that all I needed now was to be shown the mechanisms for writing this book. The book was to be a description of the spiritual evolution I have truly experienced in such a short moment in time.

I asked God how I would find the time and the resources to write this book and how it would be published. I was told to take a block of time off and travel to one of my favorite areas on the Pacific coast in Mexico. I had many excuses for not going, so of course I went. My listening was becoming stronger (and continues today).

Shortly after we arrived, I experienced some illness. I felt a lack of physical strength to persevere. My wife helped by taking dictation. This was God's plan. Her encouragement and inspirations helped make the writing easy. She was (and is) God's messenger. Yet, that is not all. As the book progressed, and I diligently practiced the meditations, many of God's messengers came to help write the book in a great variety of ways. Most had no idea they were doing so. It didn't matter. I invited them into my mind's awareness. God showed me miracles through them. God bless them as they continue on their life's journey.

Each morning, I would take a walk along the beach and the pelicans flying in formation overhead seemed to call me. Each day, I would ask God to show me the miracle in my noticing them. Their formation was flawless as they flew just above the waves looking for their fish meals. I meditated on being the pelican and felt a wonderful coordination of mind, body, and spirit in my efforts to dance with the elements in finding my meal. What a beautiful feeling of balance! Yet, I was told by the Holy Spirit there was more to this miracle. One day, I walked a bit farther to find where the pelicans nested. They showed me a large hilly area with tall cliffs. They would nest amongst the jagged rocks above the shore.

I climbed high up onto one of the hills. I climbed higher than I may have in the past since I felt the echoes of fear. Yet, they were only echoes and no longer were felt as real. As I came close to the top, I noticed these pelicans were not afraid of me. They just went about their business. I looked and identified further with them as I sat on a large rock overlooking the ocean. Suddenly I felt it. The unmistakable wind blowing in from the shore. It was powerful and cool. I became the pelican spreading my wings and easily being carried by the wind. I marveled at the ease in which the pelicans just knew this profound discovery for me. I realized I only need to be present for God's wind to take me soaring. I only need to spread my wings and let God's energy take me.

That is what this book is all about. May you soar above the waves!

INTRODUCTION

The book consists of 10 chapters, each of which describe a key concepts leading to a deeper and effortless awareness of who we really are using the eyes of God in all of our daily activities. We will see the power of love in all that we encounter, as our blocks to love fall away and we shed our unnecessary cloaks to warm ourselves in the rays of God's guiding and gracious light. We seek within to reveal the illumination of Love's childlike qualities in simplicity and faith.

Within each chapter along our spiritual path, two meditations will be offered to you, one waking meditation, and the other a guided visual imagery. These will be fully explained in each chapter. The waking meditation will be a practical way of choosing to correct our thought habits through the active use of miracles that we both co-create and appreciate as they are shown to us. The guided imagery can be practiced in a quiet spot with God's inspirational guidance. The more we are open to daily miracles, the quicker will be our relief from what we have experienced as stress; the greater the transformation to a mind open to and even expecting the blessings that God has in store for us. Can you see how joyful this all can be? All you need do is open the door and God's light shall enter!

Is it clear to you within your inner knowing self that it is much easier to have a happy day to the extent that you can keep unhappy thoughts from entering your mind's awareness? As we practice the meditations recommended in the following spiritual program laid out in the chapters of this book, we most fully find ourselves within our present NOW. NOW we can enjoy God's gifts, rather than placing our small minds within the illusion of Hell. We often create these illusions with habits of self-punishment through Guilt (past), or self-abuse through doubts of our capacity to handle what may be set before us (future). Only this moment do we have. Thoughts of past or future pre-occupations are diversions away from the glory of God's love. Free yourself from those pre-occupations and allow the constant and heartfelt companion of the Holy Spirit to walk with you in your daily spiritual journey.

The practice of loving thoughts makes each relationship in your life a Holy Encounter. This occurs as God is invited into your mind's awareness and helps you correct your perceptions of lack of love in any encounter. Decisions to seek the Voice for God in these encounters are what transform them into moments of joy and peace. So, what kind of day would you like to have? One based on the feeling of being in a cocoon, or one in which you are the butterfly, pollinating the flowers which are awaiting your instigation? And so as you give, you shall receive. As you have received, so must you give.

The following concepts are points of meditative focus helpful in transforming our minds.

- The Holy Spirit, The Voice for God
- Giving and Receiving Miracles
- Forgiveness as Salvation
- What is Creation
- What is the Child of God within
- What is the Real World
- I Am

Each concept is simply and practically explained with illustrations. The order of the spiritual path laid out in these chapters faithfully leads us progressively away from our dependence upon the attachment to our ego thought system; a system based upon perceived fears and the need for self protection. We develop a welcome reliance upon the ever-deepening awareness of our 'Child of God Within' who is our true companion in love's One connection with all others.

God bless you for your courage in what I hope will be a fascinating undertaking for you.

Chapter 1

Peace of Mind is a Decision

Teach me to put into actions my better
Impulses, and make straightforward and unafraid.
Grant that I may realize that it is the trifling things of life
That create differences,
That in the higher things in life we are all one.
And, O, Lord God, let me not forget to be kind!
-Mary Stuart

As you read this chapter, please begin your own mind retraining discipline by simply asking yourself two questions as often as you can think of them. These questions are: "Why peace of mind?" and " Why peace of mind now?" The choice we make to focus our thoughts upon these questions is a decision we make right now. It is not the kind of decision in the sense we may normally think. The decision is one of recognizing what is already ours. Peace of mind is not something we must work for or earn. It is something we already have and all the time. It is part of our package, part of being a Child of God within God. We are not choosing to make anything. We are choosing to align with everything that is God by choosing not to place clouds of worry in front of the light.

We often think that we are victims of the circumstances around us.

For many of us it seems natural to turn to thoughts based upon fearful foundations. Yet those very fears and interpretations are based on perceptions we think we see of the world outside of ourselves. This way of thinking becomes a cycle. The fear thoughts support the fearful perceptions which feed the fear thoughts. Eventually we form thought habits. When we choose to place our thought energies and beliefs in how separate we are from others, our small mindedness supports and reinforces feelings of aloneness and fear. Our aloneness becomes our reality. What we sometimes think of as emotional disorders such as depression and anxiety, are all actually variations on this conviction. And this conviction itself tends to build in strength over the years as our minds see more and more fearful events. The events seem to justify our holding onto this victim state. Maybe at some point, we even wonder if we are Children of God, or if there even is a God.

There is a way out. A true way, in fact a way so true that it has always been and always will be available for us and for everyone. With a little daily practice, you can achieve a state of mind, which has been the essence of all major religions throughout the ages. This state of mind, which you will want more and more as you experience it, is your way out of all emotional and thus spiritual feelings of discomfort. This process of claiming your rightful decision is not one of rigorous effort; in fact, it is the undoing of effort. The experience of effort requires an attachment to an end result in whatever matter appears to be troubling you. As soon as we attach, our expectations themselves place blinders on our minds. Deep inside we sense that we have closed ourselves off from the unfolding of miraculous lessons that God wishes to show us. Yet until we choose to remember our own greatness, we can keep ourselves in a small-minded frame of being. God does not wish for us to be afraid and we are never ever really alone. There is really nothing to fear.

The metaphor of light revealing truth is as universal as a smile reveals openness in greeting. When we open the shade of a window, the light that has always been there will effortlessly come streaming in.

The darkness we previously thought we were in is now immediately revealed as nothingness. Darkness is only the absence of the light that always and forever exists ready for us to open the shade of our minds. When we come to our spiritual senses, we know we have a place within our souls where God exists and where His/Her word is clear as a bell. When we are in the darkness, we may say, 'it is dark in here.' Yet, the truth would be better stated by saying, 'Light has not yet been revealed here.'

This same truth can be illustrated by our simple smile. Can we say that if a person's smile is not seen by us that the smile is not there? In but an instant, and by our request, the smile we show to another spreads and the glow of our smiles enhance each other. What we ask to place in our minds will manifest in the world we see. As we take on responsibility for our own perceptions, we are reminded again of a simple and always accurate truth. 'When I am ready to see your smile, it is because I am first ready to show you mine.' A candle never loses its brightness by lighting another.

Can you see the paradox within this framework? Our ego thought habits place the cause and thus the reality of events outside our minds. Yet, we must decide to see these events as mere reflections of what is within our minds. This helps us to choose to see God revealed through these seemingly external events. The thoughts for the Voice for God are always within our minds. The more we see the loving and Godlike qualities in everyone, the more we are able to recognize them within ourselves. The more we see ourselves as a part of God, the more we can experience where we truly exist: in the Kingdom of Heaven on earth. There boundaries of time, distance, and our possibilities are only limited by our frame of mind. We are becoming more attuned to daily miracles that show us again and again that God wants us to have it all!

Our recognizing the power of our mind's decisions moment by moment helps us choose to see the light of truth, the light of Heaven on

Earth that is always with us. To see the light is to see well beyond what appears to be external circumstances and appearances. To bask in this light is to remove blocks from faith in the form of fears and doubts of who we really are: children of God. God allows us open communication through our minds to make any event a call for love. The more love we can see around us, the more serenity and peace of mind we claim. Isn't that what we know we want? Please ponder that question for a moment.

So how do we KNOW what we truly want? What makes it so clear for us?Our knowing thoughts visit us in the blink of a Holy Instant, a time when we have tapped into the part of our minds where God resides. What feelings come to mind at the thought of a sunrise, a baby's face, a placid lake at sunset on a cool summer night, the witness of baby birds in their nest as they are being fed? In this Universal knowing we see these events as miracles of love. When you were born into your present incarnation, these ancient memories and love's gifts, which they represent, were already there within your mind. You did not have to learn your reaction to them, you simply knew. There are probably countless other examples that you can think of and I invite you to go through one day recognizing things that you know and that you have always known. This background of knowing helps us to appreciate art, to relish the smell of fresh air, to enjoy togetherness, to sense what another person feels, to share affection with our pets that speak not a word, and to have faith that our prayers will bring God's will clearly to our understanding.

Can you see that by our sharing of this sense of knowing we can witness each day as a testament of our own Oneness with God? This concept can be greatly extended, far beyond what we can imagine. Our collective thinking can literally save our world from the misery we have come to put our minds through each day. There is a well-known phrase: 'What we think expands.' This means that whenever we put our energies into what is truly real, the light of love, these thoughts will expand both within our minds and beyond to the Universal Mind which is God and of which we are a unique part. Please don't misunderstand. God's mind does not have any thoughts other than those of unconditional and everlasting love. Our part in the spreading and revealing of this love is one of faith. Keeping our hearts and minds open to see and feel the light that we know is there in God's blessings can help heal the pained hearts and minds of ourselves and of others we may never have physically met. This is the Universal loving mind of which we are all an integral part.

Is it worth it to you to train your mind in a very deliberate way to make peace of mind your habitual thought framework? Is it worth it to you to train your mind to release itself from temptations of worry and tension, and to feel direct and conscious contact with God, never alone or comfortless? And the best part is you can start with but a few minutes a day. You will feel immediate relief from stress—at first for brief periods, but then increasing in length. My hope is that you will want to increase your daily mind training as explained in the following chapters. Please use their gifts in your own way, for you are your own best teacher. With a little daily practice you will recognize the small shortcuts that you can use to form a mind set which automatically leads to mind correction. Yet, there will be times when you will find that your resistance will be strong. The habit of thought, especially ego self-protection, can be deeply engrained. The very act of questioning your thoughts can get the ego's grip on your thoughts ever tighter with fear. Simply do not allow the ego to block your awareness of your spiritual reality.

To help you along this path, treat yourself to the following daily meditation to begin your day or one similarly meaningful to you. Do this just as you are arising. Join with the Voice for God within you before thoughts of fear, anticipation, and worry begin to set you off balance. Make this statement of faith as a Child of God. Then let God through communication with you show you the power of faith and the glory of all events and encounters that come to you.

"...the quality of heart we bring to life is what matters
most.
All other spiritual teachings are in vain if we can not
love."
-Jack Kornfield, from A Path to Heart

Today, We Is One

Upon arising, stand up and see yourself in the center of a circle. Facing each direction, complete the following short steps.

Raise your hands above your head and say or think with strong conviction: 'Today, Dear God, please show me Who I Am.'

You may receive a message such as "I am a Child of God within God," for example.

Lower your hands and let the palms face the earth and say and think with strong conviction: 'Today, Dear God, show me Where I Truly Am.'

You may hear a message such as "You are in the Kingdom of Heaven on earth," for example.

Extend your arms out in front of you, palms up and say or think with strong conviction: 'Today, Dear God, show me my purpose in Your Plan.'

You may hear "Your purpose is the illumination of love, which is your birthright," for example.

Now, sit in the center of the circle quietly while seeing yourself in a world called Heaven. You need not imagine any details. Simply place the calling for that image in your mind and let it emerge through the guidance of a prayer answered. This is not an undue expectation because you are only asking to be shown what is already yours. When you see the image, thank God for reminding you of your open and continual communication with Him/Her. Then complete this meditation with the following heartfelt conviction:

'As I make no decisions without your help, Dear God, this day in Heaven will be given me. Amen.'

To release ourselves from the strain of worries, concerns and fears and anticipations. We need not think of ourselves as doing this alone. In fact, if we did feel the need to rely only on ourselves, we would be placing ourselves in the same dilemma which caused strain in the past. The core of that dilemma is the belief God is not with us. In order to achieve peace of mind, we must take the leap of faith that God will never leave us alone. In calling upon God's companionship, in achieving His/Her purpose, we become radiant in our expression of Love. It becomes a way out for us. A way out of the bonds of victimization that we tend to place ourselves in with our own small minds.

The release from our small minds and victim hood, to remembering our vast ability to join with the large universal mind, which we know of as God, is our birthright. The journey you will be taking will increase in clarity over the next several weeks. The first step is our willingness to embrace the Holy Spirit who will be our constant companion, guiding us through all the other chapter meditations. For this reason, the meditations are kept open ended, allowing much space to listen to the Voice for God, the Holy Spirit.

We will consciously train our minds through the meditations included in each chapter to see the abundant evidence of miracles, which are given to us simply for the asking. Each expression of love through the Holy Spirit becomes more evidence to expand our minds beyond the dungeons of fear and anticipation. We will find that miracles become more abundant as we consciously create them in loving relationships. We find that we are able to create miracles during the course of any encounter. We have the ability to create a moment of love between ourselves and whomever we meet.

Next, we rediscover that our relationships can bring salvation to our minds. By placing our minds in the hands of the Holy Spirit we are able to spread joy through these relationships and in turn receive what we give. At first in small spurts of time, but later in concentrated periods, we find release from tension, stress, tightness and physical pain through the concentrated release of love in our holy encounters.

As our spiritual process continues, we may expect our minds to continue to expand at an ever-steady pace. However, our thought habits do not change quickly or evenly. At this time, we need to look at our thought habits closely; specifically the habits of pride and ego. As we face the ego, we face our habit of judgment, which creates artificial, perceived barriers in our minds. There are large moments of darkness, so please do not feel discouraged. You are making progress just by staying with this program. As you continue to keep and review your journal entries, you will see the evidence of your shift in thinking. Forgiveness, as the release from critical judgment, and the awareness of God's blessings in all events, will happily visit our mind's perceptions with increasing frequency. Your journal, which is a testament to your transforming mind, is essential as a clear way of offsetting the ego. Please celebrate and share your successes as evidenced in the journal.

As we look at each one of our thought habits, we will ask the Holy Spirit for an alternative way of looking at that circumstance and situation. We will consciously ask to be released from self-abusive thinking based on fear and projection, including the fear that our minds are not changing through this discipline. We will see that every time we perceive the 'sin' of another, we have really considered ourselves as sinful, and subject to judgment, apart from and separate from others. As we progress, we allow our focus to shift away from self-criticism, and identification with and attachment to material objects that can be compared and contrasted with each other. You will notice what appears to be a subtle and simple shift occurring in your typical thinking. God's blessings, periods of joy, periods of self-acceptance, periods of gifts which bountifully come our way in the context of relationships, will increasingly show us how little we need to do to deserve our own perfection.

Ego thoughts which have increased over time, have created blocks to our awareness of the love which surrounds us; a subtle and unconscious role of victim. With the decision (in any given moment) to call upon the Holy Spirit for a new and less painful way of forgiving our past judgments, those ego thought habits can be transformed into thoughts of love. With that decision, and the resulting experience of love, we can see the miracles and look on life with a peaceful and gentle mind. It is this new way of looking at life (in the context of relationships with others, with God, and with ourselves), which is our own true salvation.

> *I was regretting the past and fearing the future.*
> *Suddenly God was speaking.*
> *"My name is 'I am". I waited.*
> *God continued,*
> *"When we live in the past, with its mistakes and regrets,*
> *It is hard. I am not there.*
> *My name is not 'I was'.*
> *When you live in the future with its problems and fears,*
> *It is hard. I am not there.*
> *My name is not 'I will be.'*
> *When you live in this moment, it is not hard.*
> *I am here. My name is 'I am."*
> *-Anonymous*

Chapter 2

Preparation for the Path Through this Book

Dear companion of my day,
You are the Holy Mystery that I surrender to when I
close my eyes.
I give you myself: the flaws, the mistakes, the petty self-
congratulations.
I give you my dear ones: my fondest hopes for them,
My worries, and my dark thought regarding them.
Take my well-constructed separation from me. Hold me
in your truth.

This day is already past. I surrender it.
When I think about tomorrow, I surrender it too.
Keep me this night. With You and in You.
I can trust not knowing anything.
I can trust incompleteness as a way.
Dark with the darkness, silent with the silence,
Help me dare to be that empty one– futureless,
desireless–
Who breathes your name even in sleep.
-Gunilla Norris, from *Being Home, A Book of Meditations*

You already have the vast majority of what you need to complete this journey. In a spiritual sense, this is not a time of learning; this is a time of remembering. We look at our ultimate goal as a re-membership without dues. We remember who we are and where we truly belong, in the conscious state of God's love.

There is an old Groucho Marx joke which is humorous because so many of us think along these lines. Groucho said, "I refuse to join any club that would accept me as a member." What makes this humorous is the awareness that we demean ourselves, thinking that we do not deserve the highest appreciation of ourselves. Groucho was saying that we are so quick to judge others, only because we are so quick to judge ourselves. Using the tools which we will describe below, we will systematically take away the artificial blocks to our awareness of the Kingdom of Heaven within.

To aid us in doing so, we may need only three tools, the first of which is not material in nature, yet very real within the core of our souls. This element is our perseverance, our willingness to seek peace of mind through a discipline of daily prayer and contemplation, in the meditations. Second, is daily journaling for the purpose of highlighting opportunities for thought corrections. (As we see our thoughts evolve during the meditations, then we have the opportunity to refine our thinking further.) Third, is joining with person or a group with whom we may share these studies. Very often the progress we make accelerates with the loving support and acceptance of those around who are sharing the walk along this path.

Expect resistance. Anything new in our lives is met with some hesitation as we expand beyond our comfort zones. It is important here is not to support and justify this resistance. When you think about it, there are things you consider sacred each day. Some of them, like brushing your teeth, you would almost never miss. Yet think how easy it would be to make excuses that our mind retraining is not sacred. We may say to ourselves that we don't have time, that we have a slight headache, that the dog needs to be walked, or there is this important phone call that must be made, and on and on. Let us see these things for what they are, merely examples of fear at what may occur should things actually change in our minds.

How often have we been willing to put something strictly to the test, carrying out the endeavor from start to finish? The discipline we are discussing in this book requires an investment of our time and energy, but consider the possible reward of peace of mind. Even a few minutes of peace a day would be worth the effort of discipline over the course of the next several weeks. Yet, if we're honest with ourselves, the greatest resistance here is the question of what we have to lose. Can we ask ourselves that very question right now before we read on? What would we have to lose by changing our thought habits? Any new behavior requires a loss of the old. As we read this book, we have begun the first step on this journey. We get more familiar with success and our ego thought system will resist that much more. Do not be alarmed by this, simply let the thoughts pass.

Each change begins with ritual. The ritual in this case is that of taking the time each and every day to join our consciousness with God. Daily meditation, prayer, and reflective journaling as described below will bring our minds back to a sharply focused purpose. This purpose is to hear the message of the Holy Spirit regarding whatever discomfort, pain or fears we believe have come our way. The discipline of ritual helps us develop a stride of willingness to continue beyond our fears, beyond our resistance. At times the ritual alone is the only reason we may take our first daily steps in our enlightenment. Only after we are well within our routine, do we feel the second wind of faith and peacefulness.

Journaling

There is nothing fancy needed in keeping a journal. All we need is the plainest of notebook paper, either bound or unbound, but placed in an order that will give us a sequence of progress. Find one spot where you will place the journal and approach it as you would your daily altar. Also, obtain a small pocket notebook in which you can make very short and simple entries pertaining to your daily spiritual excercises, miraculous expressions and holy encounters during the day. These will be more completely described in the following chapters.

Simply make it a part of your program to visit your altar where you place your journal each day. We may wish to jot down initial thoughts and intuitive impressions before and upon completion of your morning meditation, and then again in the evening. In the morning, it is often helpful to jot down brief notes on what we were shown during our meditation and what our waking daily meditation will commit us to for today. In the evening, we consult our pocket notebook entries, so we may more thoroughly dialogue with the Voice for God on what miracles were being shown us in our conscious spiritual encounters for the day.

Organize your journal using the chapter headings found in this book. Place the following entries under each day's logging: (1) your recollections of your initial thoughts and emotional state when you first woke up that morning, (2) rate yourself in a meaningful way (such as between 1 and 7) according to how easy or difficult it was for you to put yourself in a meditative state through your breathing exercise, (3) during the course of the day, what thoughts seemed to arise both during the meditations and seeming chance and/or other eventful encounters with others? We know there are no chance events. They only seem to be so. As time goes on, we will discover what we have placed in our mind will manifest itself in our daily activities.

These should not be extensive entries. What we are looking for are shifts in our thought patterns, changes in consciousness, and things that change in our perceptions, although the outward events seem to remain essentially the same. These are all significant. The more we are aware of them, the faster and more accelerated our mind transformation. Here the pocket notebook comes in handy as these miraculous events, small and large, are recorded at the time they occur. If you stick diligently to this practice, you will be amazed at all the subtle yet significant changes which are occurring in how you see yourself and the world around you, especially in relationships.

Each week review your entries for the week. Review them again when you feel you have completed each chapter as outlined in this book.

Sharing

Wherever possible, our brothers and sisters become our witnesses to our mind's changes. There is something very sacred about being able to place our thoughts into words and say them out loud. Until then, we may feel a sense of fear and trepidation, as if our mind's reflections have a twinge of elusive insanity. There is nothing insane about the discipline you are embarking upon. The insanity is remaining in the self-tortuous thought processes that many of us have taken for granted for so many years. Many of us know that we are more forgiving of others than we are of ourselves. For that reason, when we are not able to share our thought process, we run the risk of the ego attacking and discouraging this process from continuing. That is to say, it would be very easy to be critical and judgmental of our own thoughts because they are so new. By saying our thoughts out loud we achieve clarity and reinforce them. Story tellers and age old fables passed down orally before the time of the written word showed us the power of universal wisdom refined from one person to the next. An age-old remedy, we learn again and again, people are very accepting of others when speaking of matters deep within our hearts. Men and women have known for ages untold that public sharing releases much burden from our hearts and minds. As mentioned in the bible, when two or more of us are able to relate with an open mind and heart, the Holy Spirit enters automatically. We rediscover again and again, God , coming through our own feeling of empathy and compassion, witnesses a loving presence within each of us.

So, ideally, find at least one person with whom to do these exercises. A weekly study group would be very advantageous as well, because the miraculous events that become evident to us as we run through these chapters will be fascinating and very often world shattering in our minds. We need time to allow emotions to bubble up, to cry in our friend's arms, to sit quietly and hold each other's hands, to stumble over words only to discover that we know each other's meanings. We'll need time for all of this. Every event that helps clear our mind is a miracle in the context of a holy relationship as found within the group interactions.

Meditation

Meditation helps us to see how we will survive, how answers will come to us, how we will learn more of the power of our connection with the Universal Mind we call God.

There are many forms of meditation and prayer. We will describe two kinds of meditation in this book for each of the following chapters. These include guided imagery and waking meditations, both of which begin with the most basic of human endeavors, the discipline in breathing. Before we proceed with each meditation throughout this book, please practice the following deep breathing foundation.

Deep Breathing Preparation for Meditations

Find a comfortable spot where you can be reasonably sure of no interruptions. Loosen your clothing, relax your muscles the best you can. Then close your eyes. Just notice, without doing anything about it, the rate and depth of your breathing. Notice how often you take a breath and how deep the breaths are. Again, without making any changes, simply notice which parts of your body seem to move the most as you are breathing. Notice how this major movement seems to decrease as your focused attention moves away from the center of that movement. Notice any judgments you make concerning yourself for the breathing habits you are noticing. Consciously let those judgments go. Now, say to yourself "I wish to breathe consciously at this time. I wish to align my mind, my spirit, and my soul through my breathing process."

Now continue by breathing through your nostrils rather than through your mouth. Notice the coolness of the air as you are taking it in. Hear the sound of the air as it passes into you. Feel the texture of the air as it flows in. Feel your internal welcome of this life-giving force. Notice if any thoughts occur as you are consciously breathing. which you would not normally be aware of in such a deliberate and controlled manner.

As you inhale, let yourself expand your intake of air by about one second longer than normal per inhale. Whatever you do, don't strain yourself. Rather, stretch slightly what is normally your breathing habit to see if it is more or less comfortable for you. If this is not a strain for you, then maintain a slightly longer inhale.

Next, place one hand approximately one inch below your naval on what is called the solar plexus. Imagine with each breath, your hands are asking that your tummy muscles be expanded out. Feel the rise and fall of your tummy as you concentrate your movement away from the previous center of breathing, and place it squarely in that of the solar plexus. Feel the rhythm of your breathing as you begin to sense that your body goes through a deepening of conscious effort. Notice the combination of the longer inhale through your nostrils, and the extending and expanding muscles near the solar plexus. Feel the increased integration of mind and body in this effort. As you do so, think of the waves of the ocean as they rise and fall.

Now at the top of the inhale, experiment with holding your breath for about one second. Notice the feeling of suspension. If this is too uncomfortable, simply skip this step. But if not, let yourself feel the ease of control that may come naturally within these steps.

With as little effort as possible, allow the air exhale easily and naturally out between your lips. At the end of each breath, simply pause, asking yourself when the next breath is needed. Try to make that a conscious decision. As you do so, allow for the notion that you need not inhale until it is called for. Fill your mind with the reassuring thought that whenever you call for the next breath, it will be there simply for the taking.

We can see from this example of basic breathing in mediation, that there are many lessons we can learn, even from the smallest activity. When practiced several times a day, this breathing meditation allows us to recognize the nuances of our experience. We sense deeply our bond with our life sustaining force, the choices we have in life's sensory expansion. Our ability to switch thought and behavioral habits consciously through breathing, and our willingness to consider how very secure we are, vividly the integrates mind, spirit and soul.

Variation on the above meditation

If you would feel more comfortable using visualization to help keep your thoughts focused upon your controlled deep breathing, you can add this simple candle lighting element to the meditation.

Prior to beginning the deep breathing meditation above, light a candle making sure the flame is easily within your sight. Place the candle at eye level and about eight or so inches in front of you. After the first several breaths of your conscious deep breathing, open your eyes and look with great intensity at the various elements of the flame and of its movement. Begin at the top of the flame and notice the aura of heated air that emanates from the outer edges of the flame and manifests as a shimmering of the heated air. As you continue your deep breathing, let yourself feel that shimmering as if you were that air. Next, work your attention inside the flame to the bright radiance of the center of fire. Let yourself be the glowing radiance of energy. Now work your way down to the blue outline of the circle that surrounds the wick. As you see it expanding and contracting, feel your own expansion and contraction with your breathing. Finally, notice the black wick, which at times appears almost in suspension, but is really the soul of the flame. Be that soul crying for expression.

Notice how this variation allows us to focus on an eternal flame which therefore represents our eternal life. As we consciously breathe and identify with each level of the flame, our mind quiets in a combined physical and visual contemplation. For some, it is easier to block out distractions using this additional step.

Prior to doing any of the other meditations in this book, please center yourself with the initial deep breathing preparations deep breathing as outlined earlier in this chapter or any others with which you feel comfortable. The rest of the meditations will come much more easily as we allow ourselves to fall trustfully into the arms of God through these foundational deep breathing preparations emphasizing the most basic of physical energy exchange, the act of breathing shared by all living creatures.

And now, when you are ready, we can begin the path of the following chapters using the concepts and exercises we have introduced in this chapter. We can discover through this regimen, increases in personal balance of mind, spirit and soul, and an abundance of peace through awareness of our continual companionship with the universal Godhead.

True Spirituality is to be aware that if we are interdependent
With everything and everyone else,
Then even our smallest and insignificant thought,
Word, and action have real consequences throughout the
universe.

Sogyal Rinpoche

Peace Quotient Survey

As you embark on this journey, we ask that you take the Peace Quotient Survey included in the next several pages. Please be as honest as you can and notice where your mind gravitates in rating your answers. Where do you feel twinges of resistance? Where do you feel ease? At what questions is your breathing tighter? At which questions is your breathing more expansive? Which questions do you hope you will answer in a more positive manner as time goes on? Make a note of these. Take as much time as you wish by simply rating yourself from one to seven on each item; a 1 signifying total disagreement or lack of alignment in the question posed, and a 7 signifying total and continuous alignment. Again notice what thoughts of resistance may enter regarding each question. Also notice any distracting thoughts that seem to come in to pull you away from the discipline of completing the survey and contemplating the issues described.

Answer each item subjectively from 1 to 7, with 1 being "I totally disagree" and 7 being "I identify completely with the thought."

· I seek the voice of the Holy Spirit daily through prayer to help employ the means to restore my mind to where it is truly at home.

(Disagree) 1 2 3 4 5 6 7 (Identify)

· The Holy Spirit calls to me to let forgiveness rest upon my fearful dreams and restore them to sanity and peace of mind.

(Disagree) 1 2 3 4 5 6 7 (Identify)

· The Holy Spirit is God's gift, by which the quietness of Heaven is restored to me.

(Disagree) 1 2 3 4 5 6 7 (Identify)

· A miracle allows for the awakening of love.

(Disagree) 1 2 3 4 5 6 7 (Identify)

· A miracle is a gift of grace, when giving it, we receive it.

(Disagree) 1 2 3 4 5 6 7 (Identify)

· To see a miracle for what it is brings witness to the fact that God exists.

(Disagree) 1 2 3 4 5 6 7 (Identify)

· Miracles happen all the time. When we don't see them, it's because we have blocked love's presence.

(Disagree) 1 2 3 4 5 6 7 (Identify)

· To ask for a miracle implies that my mind is ready to witness it.

(Disagree) 1 2 3 4 5 6 7 (Identify)

· In his love, God shows me that I am guiltless and I am united with all Creation in that love.

(Disagree) 1 2 3 4 5 6 7 (Identify)

· I believe that when I seek the Holy Spirit that thoughts of separation can be replaced with thoughts of peace.

(Disagree) 1 2 3 4 5 6 7 (Identify)

· Salvation means letting go of illusions of differences separating us from each other and from our One Spirit.

(Disagree) 1 2 3 4 5 6 7 (Identify)

· My salvation rests in radiating the light of God to the world.

(Disagree) 1 2 3 4 5 6 7 (Identify)

· As I forgive others of what sins I am tempted to see, all my sins are forgiven.

(Disagree) 1 2 3 4 5 6 7 (Identify)

· Through forgiveness I end the cycle of masking the truth of my fellow being's Godliness

(Disagree) 1 2 3 4 5 6 7 (Identify)

· To forgive, I only need to ask the Holy Spirit to show me how, and step aside as it is done.

(Disagree) 1 2 3 4 5 6 7 (Identify)

· A sin is not a call for punishment, it is a choice with consequences which can be painful yet part of my spiritual learning.

(Disagree) 1 2 3 4 5 6 7 (Identify)

· What God creates is like God.

(Disagree) 1 2 3 4 5 6 7 (Identify)

· I am Creation, a Child of God within of God.

(Disagree) 1 2 3 4 5 6 7 (Identify)

· Creation is eternal unity with God.

(Disagree) 1 2 3 4 5 6 7 (Identify)

· Creation is the composite of all of God's thoughts, of loving infinity, which can be seen everywhere when we open our minds.

(Disagree) 1 2 3 4 5 6 7 (Identify)

· My body can be used to heal my mind.

(Disagree) 1 2 3 4 5 6 7 (Identify)

· I use my body to extend my hand to my brother as we walk along the road together.

(Disagree) 1 2 3 4 5 6 7 (Identify)

· I can only see the Real World through forgiving eyes, and a mind at peace.

(Disagree) 1 2 3 4 5 6 7 (Identify)

· When I have forgiven myself, I see only happy sights and sounds.

(Disagree) 1 2 3 4 5 6 7 (Identify)

· The real world is the symbol of my awakening.

(Disagree) 1 2 3 4 5 6 7 (Identify)

· The world I had often seen, one based on fear, is being replaced with a world based on love's visions.

(Disagree) 1 2 3 4 5 6 7 (Identify)

· I increasingly recognize that a world without love is a world without God.

(Disagree) 1 2 3 4 5 6 7 (Identify)

· When my mind is filled with truth, fear can't be present.

(Disagree) 1 2 3 4 5 6 7 (Identify)

· When I seek beyond the chains of fearful thought, I witness the truth of love's perception.

(Disagree) 1 2 3 4 5 6 7 (Identify)

· The release of my belief in fear opens my mind to eternal life.

(Disagree) 1 2 3 4 5 6 7 (Identify)

· A Child of God within of God is the Self I share with another and with God as well.

(Disagree) 1 2 3 4 5 6 7 (Identify)

· My child within remains untouched by anything the eyes observe, and remains untouched by thoughts of sin.

(Disagree) 1 2 3 4 5 6 7 (Identify)

· The Holy Spirit reaches from the child within me to all my misperceptions, correcting my thoughts.

(Disagree) 1 2 3 4 5 6 7 (Identify)

· I wish to find the Godliness in my brother's face and nothing else.

(Disagree) 1 2 3 4 5 6 7 (Identify)

· No matter what form my body takes, it is not a barrier to my loving expression.

(Disagree) 1 2 3 4 5 6 7 (Identify)

· I no longer give my body the power to override the spirit that is my true identity.

(Disagree) 1 2 3 4 5 6 7 (Identify)

- God's being resides in me.

(Disagree) 1 2 3 4 5 6 7 (Identify)

- I am a reflection of God's love.

(Disagree) 1 2 3 4 5 6 7 (Identify)

- I exemplify the word of God.

(Disagree) 1 2 3 4 5 6 7 (Identify)

- I am willing to fulfill God's role for me.

(Disagree) 1 2 3 4 5 6 7 (Identify)

- I can choose to see only the goodness in others.

(Disagree) 1 2 3 4 5 6 7 (Identify)

- I can choose to see the goodness in events as they unfold.

(Disagree) 1 2 3 4 5 6 7 (Identify)

****

Upon completion of all of your reflective studies in each chapter and the meditations included, and upon review of your journal, we ask that you take the survey again, to see what changes have occurred in your awareness of your knowing self and the Child of God within you.

Chapter 3

The Voice for God

May you lie down in peace my friend,
May you rise up full of wonder.
Wrap yourself in the One morning after morning,
O refresh your weary soul, Your only one, perfect and pure.
If you do not keep your own soul alive,
How will you welcome the morning light?
How will you welcome the morning?
Listen to the One, the song of the morning stars,
Let the One open your heart.

-Medieval Jewish Poem

This is the first step in aligning ourselves with our spiritual power. It is the only step that we must take on our own in that it is the step of inviting and calling upon the Holy Spirit, Voice for God or Universal Mind. Although the Voice for God is always present and available, God will not speak to us out of an exquisite sense of respect until we have so invited Him/Her to enter our awareness. The Voice for God is a very unique experience for each person.

Our personal relationship with God, although in essence similar, may take different forms in our minds, which make it an entirely loving one for us. For this reason, we may adopt some religious symbols or rituals to represent our communication with God. Or, we may have found that over the years the character, the essence of God, speaks to us in a way beyond and outside of any structured previous educational or religious experience. Or, we may find a blend of the two. For us to truly feel ready to get beyond plaguing thoughts of fears, anticipations, worries, and concerns, our first step here is to recognize and appreciate how God is always with us, always walking by our side.

How do we know when God is speaking to us? Actually, if you reflect back on the most awesome and intense experiences of our lives, we can recall the feeling, the essence, and the tenor of our communication with God.

Can you remember your first true awareness of God's voice? It may have been a moment of remarkable clarity in an instantaneous discovery that God was always there for you and was waiting for your invitation. Many of us learned what this experience was like when we turned to God only during a time of special importance, such as an emergency. When we invited His/Her presence into our lives, God signaled us in an unmistakable way that He/She was, is, and always will be by our side. In that unmistakable moment we became able to sense our opening to God's light.

We now recall, as in a recollection of distant past echoes, that the moment above was by far not the first moment God had been with us, for God never left us. It is the first moment when we were willing enough to be open and the first moment that we discovered one of many channels of awareness of His/Her exquisite and respectful availability to us.

What internal cues signal the Voice for God to you? The Voice for God may be a very quiet sense of knowing or it may come to you as an unmistakable whisper. In one instant, it seems a multitude of thoughts come with great clarity. God may come to us visually, or in the form of clear physical events showing us love's path. God may come to us through the words of another and we just know they are the words meant for us to hear. The form that the Voice for God takes for us depends completely upon how we are ready to receive it. Of course, we need not ask only in times of distress or great celebration. As soon as we are ready, no matter how great or small the guidance needed, God is our ready companion. It is that simple.

In virtually every circumstance leading us to feelings of discomfort, we have placed our attention upon ego fears. All fears can be reduced to one core illusion, the illusion that we are alone and not worthy of God (because of our guilt over this or that). We can take infinite comfort in always remembering what we have always known. God is around us, within us, and a part of us at all times. At any given moment we decide if we are available to the Voice for God, the Holy Spirit. This is a bit like God's radio station always broadcasting. Yet we must tune in to be able to listen.

We may know what we have just read rings true. Yet, we have many ways of entangling our minds. We think that we (and our particular set of problems) are the exception. We have seen the intervention of God in our lives throughout the years in a multitude of examples. In many cases we thought that we had come to the ultimate end of our proverbial rope. There were times when we may have felt extreme loss, we had felt abused or misused, we could not see our way clear due to of lack of resources, we felt personality flaws and felt alienated from others. We may have seen whole lifestyles change or be destroyed right in front of our faces. And yet, throughout all of this, and throughout everything that is happening in our lives today, God is still with us, and has helped see us through what we thought was the ultimate catastrophe, the ultimate loss, the ultimate proof that we could be unworthy of love. As we look back on many of these circumstances, we find that eventually, each of these seemingly painful maladies turned into a blessing, and each of these existed strictly for our own benefit.

Each challenge we survive help us to see the blocks to love that we constructed are unnecessary.

With each lesson that we learn through God and through communication with the Voice for God, we realize that survival is a state of mind and answers to our fears and to our prayers are always at hand. By deciding to remember in faith that God is always with us, communication with God can happen anytime we want, not just when we judge that our need for God deserves response. God does not put constraints upon His/Her availability to us. We have bound ourselves with thought habits of guilt and shame. Who are we to deserve to speak with God? We are His/Her children. We know our children can do nothing to cancel out our love for them. There is nothing we can do to be judged as undeserving of the love of Father/Mother God.

Our step along the path to increasing comfort and attunement with the Voice for God, through the Holy Spirit requires the use of daily preparation and many personalized methods that we will construct for ourselves to rediscover and reinforce what we know in our hearts is already there. God is with us, God will never leave us, and all that happens for our benefit.

By sensitizing our minds to listening and tuning in to the Voice for God, the presence of God will become increasingly available to us, and easier to feel within the deepest recesses of our hearts. We consciously put faith first, faith in our willingness to set aside our ego fears and replace them with a mind filled with gratitude. This step is not unlike all the other steps in which we train our minds, in that it reverses steps that our ego thought processes have habitually conditioned our minds to follow.

In our first major leap, we allow ourselves to see a dilemma, a foreboding challenge, and decide to change our habit of how we choose to respond. Now, instead of seeing the problem, coloring it with fear, anticipating the fight with potential catastrophe, we choose another way. We ask God to help us recall a short list of gratitudes from times which were similar and in which we discovered tremendous blessings from those challenges. In preparing us to hear the Voice for God, we set the groundwork with gratitude. We soon feel our minds opening, our tension decreasing. We sense the light of God. This will be the first step in our wakeful meditation.

The content of your character is your choice.
Day by day, what you choose, what you think, and you do
Is who you become.
-Heraclitus

Wakeful Meditation Step 1, the Altar

Throughout the ages people have built altars as a way of personalizing their relationship with God. When people go to their altar, they focus their mind upon the task of gratitude for all that God has previously given them. They also use this special place to find a ritual means of prayer. In this prayer, their concerns and worries are left at the altar for God to contemplate. Coming to the altar is analogous to going to a website, tuning into a radio station, or going to your community house of worship. The specific spot, the specific makeup, the specific surroundings and rituals involved are not nearly as essential as the state of mind we place ourselves in as we have approached our willingness to join with God's love rather than the ego's fear.

Perhaps when we think about an altar, we think about a place beyond doubt, beyond attack, beyond the errors and trappings, which people use to judge each other. We think about a place where what we wear or what we say is of secondary importance to what we receive through the reassurance of a special and direct line by which we can tap into God. We think of the practical metaphors of taking off your shoes before walking into a Buddhist temple, or placing a kepah on your head when walking into a synagogue, or lighting a candle in a church. Each one of these small rituals helps to place us in a particular state of mind in which we are open, ready and certain of the presence of God. We can build an altar physically almost anywhere. This can be in a formal religious institution, or it can be in a corner of a room in our own home. Ultimately, wherever we place the altar, we have used this symbol to clear a spot for God to speak with us in our own minds and hearts.

Here are some possible methods for the construction of our altar. For the physical representation of the place where you communicate with God, you may choose a particular corner of a room in your home, or at your office, or in your car; anywhere you normally frequent and visit. In this special place, there should be some objects, which are representations for you of the concepts of gratitude and eternity. Light, for example, in the form of candles, represents eternal truth. There may be objects that you have found in nature, which seem to have spoken to you in a very unique way. Or, there may be heirlooms carried down from one generation to another, things that show the continuity of your family, of your life, of the universe. How you construct your altar is extremely personal to you. Allow at least one small symbol that you would normally include on your altar to be mobile enough to be carried around with you and represent the link to that altar and to the Voice for God.

When you approach your altar, approach with thoughts only of gratitude. Like in the Buddhist temple, leave the dirt from your shoes outside. What you want to do here is relax and rest in the arms of God. Before all else, devote yourself to your daily basic deep breathing meditation as described in the last chapter. As you feel both the arms of God surrounding you at this altar, and the reassurance of God's care in examples of the past, you are coming closer to a frame of mind in which you are opening yourself to the language of God which is the language of love everlasting.

Gratitude is the reliving of miracles that have been put before us to help resolve what we thought were omens of fear and uncontrolled pain of many forms. Let us embrace the belief that whatever challenge is being shown to you now is like any other lesson that you have been shown. We had fallen into holes, yet we have been shown our way out. The lessons have helped us to be stronger and face future challenges with a more intimate awareness of God's loving intercession. So, as our first step in walking through this challenge with God's assistance, write down similar circumstances that have been resolved through your co-operative listening to the Voice for God which in turn helped you deepen your understanding of God. Although you may have felt so uptight, and even preoccupied concerning your current fears before you approached your altar, take the time to set your pain aside and do this simple exercise. Recall gratitude first and this will clear the way for clear communication with the Voice for God.

Wakeful Meditation Step 2, The Image

To personalize our discussion with God, we may find it extremely helpful to construct an image of God's holiness. We refer to that communication with God in this book as the Voice for God, or the Holy Spirit. It is our direct link to God. The more real that link is in our mind, through image and affect, the easier it is to tune in. Symbols have been used throughout eternity in the form of relics representing God and Gods, in artistic and visual representations which describe God's personality as found in religious scriptures. But no communication can be as direct as that which is completely tailor- made by ourselves. Until an article of clothing is tried on, we simply don't know if it fits. Here, we can construct our own evolving image of the Holy Spirit, making it in a heartfelt way, much more real for us.

In a quiet place, sketch your image of the Holy Spirit with your non-dominant hand. Allow it to unfold anyway that it wishes to, with-

out censoring the drawing whatsoever. It may end up being in the form
of a person, or an animal, or it might be an image which you have
never seen before. Allow the image to show itself in texture, in realism,
in character, as you might see the Holy Spirit before you. Make sure
that you draw eyes which you can look into as you communicate
deeply and sincerely. Eyes lead us directly to the seat of the soul. Over
the course of several days, refine this drawing in whatever way seems
to flow easily for you. Allow that flow to proceed without judgment.
Use colored pencils or chalk, crayons or textured means of filling in
colors for this image, or leave the colors as simply black and white. As
the image becomes more solid, see God speak to you through that
image. Now place that image in your mind. Allow it to animate itself.
After each working refinement of your evolving image of the Holy
Spirit, place it back upon your altar.

Waking Meditation Step 3, Prayer

It is now time to look at prayer. We prepare to focus our intentions
to listen to God's guidance by resonating our energies with our Universal
mind through prayer. Prayers we pick as meaningful to us can be
from formal religious training, our family traditions, inspirations from
our life's travels, or those inspired through our openness to our personal
communication with the Voice for God, the Holy Spirit. There is
certainly a wealth of prayer both written and as yet unwritten, for
words are secondary to God. All life experiences can be used as inspiration
for prayer.

There are three very simple rules to any prayer. First, we acknowledge
that God is love and only love. Second, we acknowledge that
although we are a part of God we are not the totality, therefore whatever
circumstance has caused us discomfort; we ask only that God
show us the wisdom of the unfolding of events so we can better understand
God. We expect no specific outcome; we wish to be shown only

the will of God. Third, we approach prayer with gratitude for all that God has shown us and for our willingness to include ourselves among all souls in God's universal mind. The more we can glorify ourselves by our willingness to be a part of the whole, the more we are able to make use of God's total inspiration.

Once we have brought our prayers to God's altar, we leave knowing through faith, that the answers will unfold. We commit ourselves to true vision in seeing the solution to the concerns that we have brought before God. We seek within for the strength to carry out these solutions.

Short Waking Meditation

As you go through the day, you may choose to take a small item from your altar with you, such as a picture of your drawing of the Holy Spirit, or an artifact such as a small pebble that is meaningful to you. When you are feeling tension or discomfort, you can simply reach into your pocket and feel this small object, close your eyes briefly, breathe deeply, and allowing the sensations of joining with the Voice for God to enter your mind's space. As you touch this object, imagine a key simultaneously unlocking the top of your mind, allowing a universal light to illumine brilliantly your image of the Holy Spirit. Allow that image to communicate with you in whatever way seems to be comfortable. For some people, the message of comfort and love comes in the form of words, for others it is an understanding and compassionate expression extended towards us, for others just seeing the image allows a flood of thought which we know to be Truth.

These experiences in and of themselves are healing because they help us to discern when we are open to hearing the Holy Spirit, rather than our own rather labored and demanding messages that tend to produce pressure upon the mind. In contrast, the message of the Holy

Spirit tends to be so simple and truthful, we just know that we have been given the most peaceful solution. We are called to let forgiveness rest upon our minds, knowing that in every way we will be taken care of if we follow this simple advice. Very often, the direction we are given is the one that would directly sidestep conflict, or the desire to change or control another.

These shorter, intermittent meditations, give you the opportunity to recognize and anchor the changes in our thought habits that originate in the longer morning meditations. We can place ourselves right back at our altar and to our healing communication, and tune ourselves into the presence of the Holy Spirit, showing us the most peaceful solutions in our interpersonal relationships. As these moments increase during the course of each day through our own invitation, the mystery of being at one with the Godhead becomes paradoxically both simpler and yet more awesome.

Guided Imagery Meditation

As with every guided imagery meditation in this book, we begin each morning with our basic breathing meditation. During this time, as we go down deep into our senses, we call upon the vision of our right-mindedness. In this guided imagery meditative practice, we will solidify the image of the Holy Spirit in our minds by way of invitation to the presence of God beyond words. We enhance this image, clarify it, and let it evolve in our minds.

Through our deep breathing meditation, we become relaxed and open minded. Now is the time to come physically in front of the our altar. Look at the drawing of the Holy Spirit that rests upon this altar. Breathe in that drawing as if you were inhaling it. Let that drawing melt into your being. See the details of your drawing. Notice the parts of it, especially the eyes, in which the soul of that drawing can so easily welcome yours.

When you are ready, close your eyes and see the image within your mind. Again, notice all the details that you can of the drawing. Notice the feeling of comfort and peace that continue to surround you. See the images of color that seem to emanate and notice where those colors reverberate in your body. Let the color send a ray to that part of your body where you feel discomfort. Let the energy that comes from that image directly comfort and heal whatever fears and concerns seem to be seated within that particular part of your body. Feel the rays of light from the image you have drawn as they gaze upon the emotions, the fears and concerns seated in your body in a forgiving and confident way. Allow the facial expression and the eyes to smile upon the issue that seems to emerge as you are describing your feelings in this Holy Encounter.

When you're ready, open your eyes and take in more details of the image of your drawing of the Holy Spirit. If you'd like, bring the picture down to add some details that seem to be evolving and emerging, as you meditate on the Holy Spirit breathing into your body and healing the corresponding spiritual issue emerging within your mind with His/Her infinite wisdom.

Journal Entries

Each time during the course of the day that you find a need to step back into the short guided imagery meditation as described above, please make a note concerning your search for guidance away from conflict and towards a loving heart. Use your pocket journal to note the effect this short meditative process has upon your mind. These entries should require no more than a few sentences. In the evening, these short notes can be transferred to your larger spiritual journal.

As you journal about these particular incidents, allow yourself to fall into a dialogue with the Holy Spirit. Consciously 'hear' how to give your fears and your resistance over to the call for love (as you may now understand it) from the other person. Let the writing be spontaneous and as long or as short as is needed. At whatever point you first wish to stop writing, continue writing just a short while longer. This will signal the stepping into what might have been an area of some resistance. Don't go to the point where you are feeling strained, simply stretch your comfort zone, ever so slightly.

Affirmation to be said and thought as often as you are inspired:

"The Voice for God, the Holy Spirit, is my constant companion through times of challenge."

When it is time to move on:

When you feel that you have been able to do the following with some ease, then go onto the next chapter.

- Construct a personally meaningful altar and visit that altar daily.
- Take into your heart the complete image of the Holy Spirit, which you have drawn and refined.
- Develop a pattern of short meditations which ask for God's guidance; visualizing your drawn image, which is increasingly being clarified in your mind.
- While transferring your experiences into your spiritual journal, you are able to discern through active dialogue with the Voice for God those messages of peace and love versus the messages, which cause ego-based discomfort.

Continue with these daily practices as we move into the next step of our spiritual path.

A voice asked,"who is God?"
Soon after the pine trees signed softly..."I am"
And deep in the jungle of grass and weeds, a tiny ant
paused and declared
"I am."
From a million light years away, the burning answer of a
star came.
"I am."
A turtle poked its head out of its shell and said,
"Oh, I am."
The ocean roared,"I am."
The trees softly swayed, "I am."
A little newborn child cried, "I am."
A yogi high in the Himalayan caves chanted, "I am."
The voice was frustrated. Exasperated.
This time its question was insistent:
"Will the real God please stand up?"
And the entire universe stood up!
-Hilda Charlton

Chapter 4

Discovering Miracles

Above all else then, be prepared at all times
For the gifts of God and be ready always for new ones.
For God is a thousand times more ready to give
Than we are to receive.
-Meister Eckhart

Miracles have a meaning beyond what is commonly used in our everyday life. Miracles occur strictly within our minds. They are every day events and herald the presence of God's love around us in every waking moment. A miracle is a gift of grace, and when recognized as a gift of mind correction, freely given to us through the Holy Spirit, their abundance becomes increasingly clear to us. Miracles need not be sensational in nature as they are simple, bright moments in our daily existence. We can receive miracles by noticing them around us and we give miracles as we develop moments of joyful encounter with others.

A miracle is a mind correction that more clearly shows us how to recognize love's blossoming. Miracles take everyday events and make them open to a deeper understanding of the blessings that are in our lives at any moment. Since these blessings are all around us everywhere and all the time, there are no conditions required for miracles to happen, except our open mindedness to perceive them. Our awareness and recognition of these miracles reaffirm for us continuously our deserved nature to be shown opportunities of joyful love.

Miracles undo errors of criticism and self-judgment that tend to cloud our minds. A miracle can occur in a moment in time seemingly unrelated to the events around us. As a means of allowing the Holy Spirit to show us how to better open our minds, miracles are a means of intervention on behalf of our own peace of mind. They are the bright moments that we allow to shine beyond the clouds of ego distraction. Miracles are as simple and natural as the shining of the unpretentious sunlight, as far reaching as our minds will allow and as penetrating in reassuring spirit as the sunlight's warmth upon our bodies. In a sense, the miracles around us help bring the little sparkles of joy in life, which help remind us that many of the fears that we think are so real are transitory and exist only as long as we give them energy. Miracles show us the everlasting and constant place of blessed moments. They show us the miraculous unfolding of God's guidance through the Voice for God.

Miracles are universal. In order to see and experience miracles, we need only be willing to ask for them to be shown to us. This is where our awareness of the Holy Spirit is so necessary. Each miraculous moment is called a Holy Instant, for a miracle needs no framework of time to show itself to us, and if one passes unnoticed from our awareness, we only need look again and the next one will be there for us to see.

Miracles are universally understood by those who see them for their innate tenderness, simplicity, and loving images. No matter where you are sitting at any given moment, miracles are happening around you. Miracles shine God's loving light to help us fully experience the truly meaningful things in our surroundings, such as the beauty of nature, the warmth from a fireplace on a cold winter's day, the distant call of life such as birds singing to each other, children playing, people chatting.

Colors that are ever present, register in our minds when we truly let ourselves see them. A flower will bloom following God's plan. When we choose to look at the flower, we can see many miracles unfold for us from many different angles. As we contemplate the many petals of the flower as shining from moment to moment in the sunlight, each angle combined with each ray of sunlight that touches upon the blossoms shows us a gift and a blessing unto itself. Any miracle is holographic. Each part, as well as the combined whole, has a message of infinite love fully encompassing its essence.

Miracles can be moments enjoyed again and again as they are relived in our minds for their precious quality. A miracle can be enjoyed to the extent that we tune in and appreciate it. Using this orientation, miracles happen all the time, to help brighten our minds and to reassure us of everlasting life, of which we are a part.

Miracles are abundant. We can continuously sustain our minds with miracle moments. There are more than enough for our minds to everlastingly appreciate. We balance ourselves emotionally and spiritually by our willingness to take in and sustain ourselves with these miraculous blessings from which we can pick at any given time.

We invert perception with miracle awareness. Our minds take the common, and make it spectacular, not in physical terms, but rather with joy which miracles bring us. Events that seem to be hard and pressing, become easier and smoother. We consciously, interlace miraculous moments into our awareness, to neutralize, lighten, and defuse the times when our egos bring up thoughts of strain and anticipation of what may forebode. Miracles bring us back to the only time there is, the present. Stress and anxiety come from ignoring miracle moments. Yet, we can continue to choose to fill our minds with the invitations to the real world, the world of eternal love that miracles bring to us.

Our consciously taking in the miracles that are happening around us is what this particular step of our spiritual practice is about. Miracles are an on-going interchange. Once our mind is corrected through receiving miraculous perceptions around us, we feel a sense of joy, which brings a desire on our part to interaction with others around us in a likewise joyful manner. Love, humor and light spread effortlesslessly and make things easier for everyone around us. In this chapter, we will look at meditative exercises that help us to recognize our miracles.

Hope is an orientation of the spirit
An orientation of the heart.
It is not only the conviction that something will turn
out well,
But the certainty that something makes sense,
Regardless of how it turns out.
-Vaclav Havel

Waking Meditation

Upon completion of your daily deep breathing meditation outlined in Chapter 2, practice receiving miracles. Begin your meditation by asking the Voice for God for the recognition of at least three miracles that have recently manifested in your life. You need not concentrate extensively on these, simply let the thought that is requested extend out into the universe and then allow the answer to emerge. As you do this, think about the blessings that have been shown you. See them in your mind. See the people involved. See the circumstances involved. During the course of the day, reaffirm these blessings when you encounter those persons.

As you go about your daily preparation to greet the day, doing the seemingly mundane things, ask the Holy Spirit to be open to the sensation of the miraculous. Let yourself see the miracles, feel the miracles in the form of blessed sensations. Let the small events that happen have a high and bright impact upon your mind . For example, miracle sensations can be found in the simple drinking of your cup of morning tea. We can hear the sound of the water boiling, feel the light steam as the liquid is poured, the slowness of your breath as you settle into drinking from that cup, the slightly full feeling of ingestion from the liquid, and the care and the interest that you take in discerning the taste with every sip. The blessing of such an event can be so simple in its joy. Each seemingly mundane or small event is filled with miracles and we can find examples at every turn. We only need expect them, and increasing moments of our existence become moments of awe, wonder and reassurance of the power of the Voice for God.

In our shorter waking meditations, we practice miracle discovery. During the course of the day, we can notice larger areas in our waking life that can be a source of many miraculous moments. When you are ready, pick at least two a day and break them down into miraculous blessings that are yours for the noticing. The example of the cup of tea above, describes this process. The noticing of the miracle can be momentary, or can extend for a few minutes depending on your time schedule. Think of these moments as mini-vacations giving your mind a short release. When we look at investment in time in the whole picture of our days, we see just how very little is required to release tension.

During these concentrated moments of miracle mining, simply pull out your pocket notebook, write a few words about what event, circumstance and/or situation you have used to draw out your miracle perceptions and sensations. Then rate your state of mind after you have taken the time to mine the miracles. Use a simple method of reflecting on your level of peace of mind, such as less tense/more tense, or using a rating scale from 1 to 7 (with 1 being least and 7 being the most) ; recalling the tension before you took the time out and the rating afterwards.

The relief that we feel will be at first short-lived yet with each additional gift of miracles exploration that we give ourselves, we will find our minds remain increasingly released from the strain that comes from holding on to problems, anticipations, guilt and fears which our ego thoughts seemingly call 'reality.' We feel a much greater state of overall peace during our days as we consciously opt for the Universal Mind of which we are an everlasting part. It is the Kingdom of Heaven on earth, our true reality which we often, sadly, ignore. Now we can ask ourselves why. We can decide to change our minds this very instant.

Guided Imagery

Upon completion of your deep breathing meditation in the morning, ask the Voice for God to show you the vision of a beautiful special place, which treats your senses. Do not conjure up this place on your own, but rather, in asking the Holy Spirit to show you this place, allow whatever scene or images emerge. You may at first question what you are being shown. Do not try to control the images, however. Do not try to expand upon them, or alter them in any way. Your only conscious task in this guided imagery is to keep an open mind and discover what is shown to you.

You will find the sense of time will slow down for you during the course of your guided imagery, and you will notice details of things and details of the details. You will see both simplicity and enhanced awareness. Your heart will be lifting. Continue with this guided imagery for as long as it is comfortable. Maintain your deep breathing as you continue to ask to be shown the scene, the sensations, and the unfolding of the miracles through the Voice for God.

Initially, the time period for the guided imagery meditations will seem short. This is a process that is developing within you. You will have a sense of knowing when the time for guided meditation is done. Don't fight that intuition.

Journal Entries

Immediately after these meditations, jot down in your small note-book, your subjective rating of your state of peacefulness, a few key images which arose and any key ideas on the slowing down of percep-tion, and miraculous details. At the end of the day, transfer the short notes that you have made of your miracle mining from your pocket notebook into your journal. As you do so, openly dialogue with the Voice for God as you re-member the benefits of a balanced mind. Describe both the images and experience that you had as you dialogue with the Voice for God in your journal using these notes.

Let the guided imagery tell you a story as you are writing about it. Let it show you those thoughts sensations, interests the Voice for God would have you expand in your daily and waking life. Notice whether any messages received in your meditation had application during the day. If you're unclear of the lessons that are being shown to you, sim-ply write the question: "What lesson would you have me see as you've guided me through these images?"

An answer will come to us. We need not use contemplation. As we write down those images that we seem to gravitate towards, we see these as God's invitation to use our more expansive awakening con-sciousness in our daily lives. Increasingly, we use our awareness of the miracles to more clearly hear the Voice for God .

Affirmation to be said and thought as often as you are inspired:

"Dear God, open my mind that I may see your reflections of love given unto me."

When it is time to move on

·   The identification of miracle perceptions in seemingly small events in everyday life.

·   The recognition of a clear, balanced state of mind from miracle interactions.

·   Guided imagery allowing the Voice for God to show us in metaphor how we can notice miracles more easily.

·   The ongoing entry in our journal of these miracle interactions.

After having completed to your satisfaction the above skills, you will be guided to know when to go on to the next chapter in your spiritual path. This chapter will help you discover the radiance we feel as we give miracles through our own Co-creation.

Life is this simple: we are living in a world that is
absolutely transparent
And God is shining through it all the time.
God is manifest everywhere and in everything-
In people, and in things, and in nature, and in events.
God is everywhere and in everything and we cannot be
without God.
It's simply impossible.
-Thomas Merton

Chapter 5

The Giving of Miracles

Geese appear high over us, pass and the sky closes.
Abandon, as in love or sleep, holds them to their way,
Clear in the ancient faith: what we need is here.
And we pray, not for new earth or heaven, and in eye
clear.
What we need is here.
-Wendell Berry

The last chapter shows us that we are surrounded by miracles. Miracles are not the unusual; they are the natural course of events. When we don't see them, it's because our mind is clouded. The clouding comes in the form of fear, self-protection, guilt, worry, and other unnatural states of mind and emotions. As we proceeded to do the exercises in the last chapter, it may have become clear to you that the more you expect miracles, the more they appear. This is what we can loosely call the receiving end of miracles. To receive a miracle, we simply pay attention to what is going on around us. We open our minds and hearts to the blessing that the Voice for God presents to us.

The fact that these events themselves touch a joyful tone in our hearts is a demonstration of the universal nature of the Child of God within us all. The blessings that are miracles can put a smile on the face of people of all ages, of any origin or cultural affiliation, or of any background. When we hear a bird singing, we feel a sense of calm. We listen very closely to that song, as if we ourselves are the receiver. When we see the expression on a cat's face, our hearts melt, as if the cat were smiling and looking into our eyes in particular. All of these represent an infinite moment of moments where we allow ourselves to experience miracles.

The other side of miracles has to do with our claiming responsibility for the state of our own minds. We are also the creator of miracles. We take the energy of miracles and allow it to pass through us to others. We complete a process which not only brings joy and attentiveness to others with whom we encounter, but also multiplies God's blessings.

Together, miraculous thoughts fill our minds as we collectively share our miracle energy. To be able to give miracles requires no special effort. It is simply a matter of paying attention to what we have allowed into our minds, and then with faith in how they will be received, we spread the Good News that love's energy can be freely given and received. This can be done through words, gestures, kind mannerisms, or just thoughts of grace and gratitude. Miracles know no special media. What we fill our minds with will simply spread to others.

This is what is meant by the expression that what we give, we receive, and that giving and receiving are the same. Love freely given becomes very attractive in its expression. When we choose to give love's energy, we soon receive kindness, friendliness, and warmth either from the receiver or from places we did not expect. It is like a boomerang effect. What we give out will return. God will show us the way best for us.

The giving of miracle energy has a double benefit. It corrects the minds of those who are in receipt of the miracles and secondly we see the world of relationships in a much easier and less distorted fashion. When we expect miracles, the Child of God within jumps for joy at the anticipation of new folks to meet, to share candidly what is already around us, God's blessings. As we have done the exercises in the last chapter, we have come to realize the abundance of miracles already around us. As we continue to do them, we will find greater and greater abundance. This helps balance our minds and place them in a greater sense of clarity. By the very nature of concentrating on miracles that we perceive around us, our minds spend more time in a corrected state. The conscious act of giving the energy we receive through our openness to miracles enhances this effect that much more.

Here is an example. Who amongst us has not run across an injured animal unexpectedly? Remember the automatic feeling of compassion which welled up inside of you. The pain that animal felt, you too may have felt in a small way. This is quite automatic. If you're like most folks, you had a desire to reduce the suffering of that animal. This may have very well been in the form of getting help for the animal, or at least making it more comfortable.

The giving of that aid to the animal, both in thought and in actions, become a state of mind that we can recall even at this moment. Our being present for that animal at just the right time and at just the right spot was a miracle. Even if we were not able to 'do' something to reduce this animal's suffering, our presence reduced the fear just a bit and allowed the animal to either be helped physically, or to move on in its journey.

What were those moments like in our mind? What made those moments to be both unique and a cause for pause from the rest of our daily plans? It was more than compassion. It was a moment of true joining with all life and all of its beautiful interconnectedness. We knew we could communicate beyond words to let that animal know that although we had never previously met, we have always known each other in the most spiritually intimate way. These are moments in time when we know that our being there with that animal, or that person, is the most noble thing we can do.

What other ways can you think to give miracles? What other ways can we find to multiply the feeling of peace and joy in our lives as we translate the miracles that we have received in our minds to express love for others? There are a variety of ways to do this, many of which we discover with practice, focus and interest. They seem to fall into a few categories.

First, we can fully take the joyous sensation of miracles, and ask the Holy Spirit to help us find opportunities to spread this light energy. We may spread this energy to whomever is shown to us, in whatever way is given us. We may pray for open mindedness and clarity of communication with the Voice for God in behalf of a particular person whose thoughts and experiences have come to us. We can also give from our own abundance in small physical and emotional ways. Any way we may join our minds through empathy, words, or physical kindness helps alleviate the suffering of the other person, bringing us to greater fulfillment of our purpose and theirs. These Miracle moments spread love energy to the whole.

A miracle given is a spiritual expression changing our focus away from physical or emotional suffering. Miracles can be given freely through general kindness. We can give a flower to a stranger, or to a loved one, to help symbolically communicate the blessing of love. This, I like to call the spreading of our awareness of Heaven on Earth. Whenever we are able to convey a general feeling of calm and serenity in a conversation, it is because we have attuned ourselves to the Child of God within us and within the others.

We can look beyond adult words and expressions and see only the children inside us all, asking to be loved. We can feel the same compassion as we see an injured animal, or when holding a baby child in our arms.

Our desire to join with the Holy Spirit within our hearts attunes us to the miracles of our relating as ever- present soul mates. Without saying anything in particular, or doing anything at all that can be physically seen, our inner peacefulness comes from seeing the miracle of the other person's holiness. That unconditional regard, with total absence of conflict is what we are seeking. It makes every relationship a holy encounter. Assuredly, our peacefulness spreads to others in any conversation, regardless of the topic. Peace is what we all want. In fact, it is our natural state of mind. Being 'right' does not in itself bring us peace, yet an atmosphere of peace will always draw out the right solution.

We begin to see just how great our spirit is through our giving of miracles. It is not only eternal and infinite, but it is energy far beyond quantification and far beyond physical expression. We are the Children of God.

What a caterpillar calls the end of the world,
The Master calls a butterfly.
-Richard Bach

Waking Meditation

Upon completion of the morning breathing meditation at our altar, we ask the Holy Spirit to place in our minds on one or more relationships to focus upon during the day, that may be a recipient of our simple act of kindness. Ask the Holy Spirit what form that might take, whether it be a kind word, a gesture, a favor, or another form. When the form occurs to us we write it down in our pocket notebook. On our way to work, or wherever we meet this person, we think about the manner in which our kindness can be communicated. Our connection completes our commitment to doing and being a messenger of a miracle moment. We feel within our mind and our heart center an immediate connection that we establish with this person. We send this person our goodwill and love.

We savor this gift given and received. Whether we are with that person physically or not, we can tune into their mind and spirit through the Universal Mind consciousness that we call God. We have faith what we have done out of love will be well received, if not for the form of the gift, from the giving itself. We feel this moment of love and joy we both share without ego strings attached.

At first we may hesitate to give of ourselves, since we may not feel worthy to be a messenger of God. We take faith, we are much more precious than we may currently realize. Only by these acts of giving do we come to recognize just how easily we can bless the world whose arms are extended, waiting for our embrace. We find once we have reached out to our fellow human being in this manner, we immediately feel a heightened sense of awe and serenity, which is the presence of the Voice for God smiling within us.

We can do several of these each day. The short version of this waking meditation is to keep in mind, throughout the day, the desire to give miracles, and then, as we are shown these opportunities, we simply take them. Miracles need not be great and vast. They can be momentary thoughts and gestures inter-connected. And thereby, fear slips away. In a sense, miracles bring us to a point of timelessness. Although we appear to be separate, we have never really left each other or our creator.

Guided Imagery Meditation

Upon completion of your deep breathing morning meditation, see yourself sitting in an area such as a garden in which there are many beautiful sensations. Feel the joy of the rhythm of bright music in the background. See your image of God as you have drawn it, and see this image upon your altar.

See the little faces of angelic messengers hovering over and around you and coming to you by way of light, energy, warmth and love. See them emanating from the universal life force which we draw from readily. Let them fill your being, your heart, and your spirit.

Let the energy rise to your heart and swirl into your mind. Let your mind fill with a radiant glow of light. Feel the light; see the light in your mind. Feel the composite of an infinite number of faces which have come to you, and let the light shine from all corners of your mind upon these fellow children of God. Free yourself from concern of where this energy goes. Claim the assurance of love's infinity. Simply feel the power of the light of love coming effortlessly into you, rising and building within you, and radiating and glowing out from you.

Now simply ask these three significant questions:
· Who am I?
· Where am I?
· What is my purpose?

Journal Entries

When you can, jot down in your pocket notebook, those moments when you are inspired to give miracles. Later, in the evening, as you dialogue with the Holy Spirit, relive the effect giving miracles has upon your mind and thoughts. Write down any changes you perceive. Then answer the three questions above without contemplation. Simply allow the Holy Spirit to answer with you in the light of miraculous opportunities you have created.

Affirmation to be said and thought as often as you are inspired:

> *"Today let me feel, Dear God, I am the*
> *light of love."*

When it's time to move on:

Practice with concentrated effort, giving and receiving miracles daily, spontaneously directed by the Holy Spirit . When you feel this is becoming comfortable for you on a daily basis, you will have completed among others, the following tasks:

- Filling our mind with God's abundant blessings and manifesting these blessings in a way focused and specific to everyday Holy Encounters
- Increasing the amount of time during the course of our days where our minds are filled with peace and joy of giving and receiving miracles.
- Releasing prayerful good wishes to those whom we may not have seen or known physically.

In the end, you are your own best guru— your life is your
guru.
As you need them, special individuals may appear
To help you find the road that leads to the road.
But these are not your only teachers.
Everything that happens to you is your teacher.
The secret is to sit at the feet of your own life
And be taught by it.

-Polly Berrien Berends
from Coming to Life

Chapter 6

Forgiveness, Our Salvation

It makes no difference how deeply seated may be the
trouble,
How hopeless the outlook, how muddled the tangle,
How great the mistake;
A sufficient realization of love will dissolve it all.

-Emmet Fox

We have been able to see in the last several chapters, peace of mind depends strictly on the way we see and treat the world. Peace of mind depends upon our state of mind, and our state of mind becomes a simple yet sometimes elusive awareness of decision for loving perception. From moment to moment we can choose to maintain our peace of mind. We choose to fill our mind with love's awareness rather than allow alternative ego thoughts. Regardless of what situation or relationship we find ourselves in, our simple choice is one of this moment's salvation.

There are several ways of approaching the choice for salvation. We can tune into our body and mind as we go through the day, noticing any moments when we are feeling discomfort, tension or strain. These are signals that ideas of fear have replaced those of love's potential. If you look at any such thoughts, you will probably come up with phrases like "but look at what they've done to me," or "if I don't do something about this, then a harmful thing will happen." or "this time/event or circumstance is simply too overwhelming for me to handle." There are many other such comments that you can hear your mind speaking when you're feeling discomfort. They all boil down to fear and fear is a lack of faith.

Put another way, all events that come our way challenge our spirit to recognize our willingness to decide for salvation. How willing are we to look at any event as an opportunity for us to see again the guidance that God provides us? With our open mindedness, all events, big or small, will guide us toward greater wisdom and the greater ability to see love's lessons in future relationships. What is put in front of us need no longer be a scary prospect, but rather one of mild curiosity. What does God wish to show me this time? How may I be so blessed? We can place foremost in our mind the conviction of our own continual salvation.

Relationships provide an arena for opportunities to choose salvation for our peace of mind . Although these relationships seem to differ in form, they all have a very large common denominator. They are opportunities to bring in the guidance of the Voice for God when we feel discomfort around what we may see as misunderstandings or disagreements. These too, for a wide variety of reasons, can lead us into the temptation of discomfort, a desire to take control, and the hopes of influencing or manipulating others so the relationship will go in a direction that we think would be less fearful. Any time that we attempt to control a relationship, we have actually entered into an unholy event in need of healing.

Discomfort in a relationship often happens when we block our mind's heartfelt listening to the message of love our companion is showing us and instead we impose on that relationship what we expect it to become. We call this a 'special relationship' because instead of acting as equals, one of us is acting as if the relationship is here especially for them to make what they invent it to be. This is a clear example of ego, that is, the Edging of God Out of our relationship. This nightmare always results in greater fear, not less for both parties. Our expectations may overshadow what the other person has to offer us.

Our own ego imaginings always overshadow the loving essence of the relationship as it may truly unfold. We may deprive ourselves of what holy lessons about ourselves and our spiritual growth that can come from this relationship. Like riding on a wild horse, we can only join with the ride by giving both parties free rein. Only in loving and exquisite appreciation can the spirits involved find a way of connection, influenced by the freely invited presence of the Voice for God.

Have you ever had a verbal contest, which ultimately amounted to point/counterpoint on who is most right or who is least to blame? Any perceived need to be right or even 'more right' is based on judgement. We are imposing our view of righteousness upon the innocence of our brother/sister. Can we see how these disagreements imprison our own minds? The whole feeling of rightness presumes the other party to be wrong. When I am 'right' and you are 'wrong', we are lead to feel very 'different' or separate from each other. For that moment we have turned away from the only reality, awareness of our oneness in love's connection.

Your companion wishes to learn from you, and as we open ourselves to learn from them, instantly, the atmosphere changes to one of peaceful salvation. There is never justification for placing our attention on differences. When we choose salvation, we choose to be totally open minded to what the other party can offer us by way of information, reflection, miracles and loving support. So, the next time that your partner spills coffee on your lap, choose to see a loving understanding for the error and an opportunity to clean it up together.

The decision to give and receive miracles helps us as an incentive to choose to decide for our own mind's salvation. Recently I saw a couple who described their marriage was closer than ever after over 50 years. When I asked what their secret was, the husband answered that as of late, he had become very hard of hearing; therefore, he literally did not hear points of controversy, as he would perceive them. Our mind's salvation is a choice to choose away from conflict when we begin to feel uneasiness. We don't have to make this choice alone. We have said before, the only step we need to take on our own is the choice to ask for the Holy Spirit, the Voice for God to enter into our present moment of awareness, our present moment of relationship.

Another example of how we learn through relationships is found in our conscious awareness of our mind's projections. Projection is the reflection of our mind's concept of itself upon the world we see. Like a mirror, these reflections can be loving or unloving forms of thought. Our companion becomes the projection mirror of our minds current self-concept. Whether we see joy, love, and happiness in our moments with another person, or we see conflict, pain, and misunderstanding, any and every aspect of our relationship experience has originated in our own mind's projections.

We can look at our relationships as a way of noticing how often we choose to see the Kingdom of Heaven within that relationship. Relationships which are only loving, kind and joyful reflect a mind nestled in God's light. A relationship, on the contrary, which is tense, shows us a mirror reflection of how we ourselves have placed fear above the altar of God. This is especially hard for many of us to face because we would like to think that which we see happening outside of us can't be controlled by us. Yet, as we have seen in the chapter on miracles, we can see what we choose to see in any event. Of the thousands of things that are occurring in any given moment around us, we choose to see only a very select few. Each of these awarenesses are filled with opportunities to see miracles. Any aspect of a relationship that we think initially is outside of ourselves and within another is really our mind's projection of what we need to look at within ourselves.

The mechanism to travel deeper into God's lessons for us is forgiveness. Forgiveness, as used here, is a frame of mind that helps us to recognize that what we thought the other person did has really not occurred with the judgments and projection that we have placed upon it. Forgiveness is not a form of pardon; instead it is a form of blessing. We overlook our temptation to judge and excersize our humble awareness of how a challenge can help us to heal from our hurts and open ourselves to our natural state, a mind of God's peace and love. Our forgiveness truly lives through the concept "do unto others as you would have them do unto you." Who among us does not feel better when we take a mistake, learn from it, and release ourselves from guilt that would otherwise hold us back from picking ourselves up and starting over? In seeing the unshakeable falseness in any need to punish or be punished, forgiveness is a bridge to the Kingdom of Heaven in a relationship.

Forgiveness is our state of mind making the loving decision to consciously choose to help our fellows through compassion rather than judgment.

We decide to treat our fellow human being in the faith that God will show us the way through any misunderstanding. Whatever errors in withholding love will eventually become clear to us along our spiritual path. If we are called upon to walk with our brother/sister for a time in the midst of their suffering or joy, we can be sure of learning from what we see of ourselves in them.

To deny forgiveness is to pass judgment on another and withhold from us the gift of understanding. An unforgiving mind protects projections, tightening the chains of our own victim-hood. Our own ways of hiding from ourselves through projection become more veiled and harder for us to discern, thus less easily accessible to our own reflections through the Voice for God.

Unforgiving, projected thoughts tend to take up a great deal of space in our minds. They have the curious nature of taking control until we ask to see our fellows in the light of love. Whenever we feel discomfort, we can ask for another way of viewing how another person has treated us or treated others. The Voice for God, the Holy Spirit will show us the way beyond any perceived differences as we listen. This is our conscious act of forgiveness.

A forgiving mind stands back from a situation in which there appears to be a wrongdoing and remains still, quietly doing nothing, while consulting with the Voice for God. It stops itself from jumping to offense, attack or self-protection. Such a mind merely looks and empties itself so that the Holy Spirit might give a loving interpretation of the other person's call for love. Without forgiveness, we fall into judgment. Forgiveness can be a welcome and discerning alternative in our minds whenever we feel tightness or the slightest amount of irritability. When we ask for forgiveness, the Voice for God will always answer, therefore this is not a step that we have to do alone. We, in turn, are always forgiven for errors that we make as we forgive others. What relief we feel as we remember more deeply that God is a forgiving God! Now it is time for us, as Children of God, to share that very function, to open ourselves to the innocence in our own reflections and in our perceptions of others.

> *"Whoever has a heart full of love,*
> *Always has something to give."*
> *-Pope John XIII*

Waking Meditation, Part 1

Upon completion of the morning deep breathing meditation, make a short list of two or three areas in which there may be a point of controversy in relationships anticipated in the day's events. Simply read over your words and with each phrase that you have read, say the following affirmation:

'This event/relationship/concern need not happen in a fearful frame-work. God, I ask that you show me only a peaceful and loving solution. Even if we differ in our opinions, may I relate to you from the place in my mind where my Child of God resides.'

As you say these words, after each phrase, take several deep breaths, opening your mind and digesting their full appreciation.

Next visualize your approach with each individual referenced in your phrases. Begin your encounter with a clear meeting of your eyes and a smile. Record in your notebook the level of discomfort rating from one to seven as you contemplate your meeting. Place the faith in a peaceful solution first.

Then rate, from one to seven, your emotional state after having spoken the affirmation above, and again after visualizing these meetings.

Waking Meditation, Part 2

As you go out to physically meet these people, use your earlier visualization as a reference of your intention. When actually having the face-to-face encounter with the person(s) with whom you had antici-pated possible tension, meet the eyes of the individual as often as pos-sible. When feeling tempted to defend, convince, or assert your own orientation, step back in your mind and ask the Holy Spirit, the Voice for God, to show you a peaceful solution, at least at the moment. Some-times this requires simply saying nothing or letting the other party know that at this point, you have to think about the matter before you. Or you might find that understanding and accepting the other party's point of view is a first step in looking toward your own resistance to being open to the lesson being shown through this relationship.

Next, as you are in the midst of this conversation with the other person(s), imagine this person(s) to be yourself. Imagine that you are they and you are taking on their point of view. Notice as you place yourself in this position, how clear your own resistance to seeing their call for love, has been in your mind.

After completing your discussion, think about those fears and irritations that you had previously anticipated would block love and understanding of the other party. Contemplate whether or not those fears came to pass, or whether you were successful in seeing their point of view. Jot down a few key phrases in your small notebook for later contemplation.

Short Waking Meditation and Affirmation to be said and thought as often as you are inspired:

After completing your evening journal entries of the above encounters, review them one more time, and envision the face of the person involved. Then, say the following:

"I bless you for all you have taught me about myself and about my union with God."

Guided Imagery Meditation

Upon completion of your deep breathing meditation, bring your anticipated grievances of difficult interactions to your altar. These grievances may be symbolized as carried in a heavy bucket you bring to your altar. Feel the weight of this bucket. Feel the weight upon your mind and upon your spirit. Then ask the Holy Spirit what makes it so difficult for you to see a way of loving these persons. Look deeply into the face of the Holy Spirit. Let the Holy Spirit empty the contents of the bucket and as he/she does so, see a radiant light illuminating the lessons that the Holy Spirit wishes to present to you.

Look into that light. Ask the Holy Spirit to show you the similarities between yourself and the other parties involved. Let the Holy Spirit show you in little mini-scenes, ways in which you have acted similarly to what you anticipate of the other party. As you keep your mind open, allow the face of the Holy Spirit that has been placed upon your altar to merge with your own. See it transform in your mind. Allow the Holy Spirit to show you who you really are.

Don't let yourself force any of these awarenesses. If they don't come immediately, then it's a sign that you may not be ready as yet. Enough will come to give you just the number of lessons that you need for that day. Don't let yourself be talked out of what you have seen by your ranting ego thoughts. Once completing the meditation, jot down in your notebook a few key phrases that you heard and sensed from the Holy Spirit. In the evening, when you do your journal entries, dialogue with the Holy Spirit on how you may alternatively see such qualities in yourself transforming and changing. Express your deep appreciation to the Holy Spirit.

Journal Entries

Reflect on your ratings of comfort/discomfort as you anticipated your particular encounters identified in your morning waking meditation. Then look back on the ratings you noted after the actual encounter. In the evening, write about each one of these meetings in your journal. Dialogue with the Holy Spirit on how your opening to faith in a peaceful solution, one unhampered by past recollections or future anticipations, has helped your mind see this relationship anew. Rate your emotional state as you write about your ability to call upon the Holy Spirit in the name of peace and your mind's salvation. Dialogue with the Holy Spirit on what fears and anticipations you are willing to surrender as you see these persons again as you would see yourself.

When it's time to move on:

You will want to work this step on its own for some time, as many opportunities for learning forgiveness through relationships will be offered to you. When you are moved to do so, you will return to the meditative exercises. Each time, you will find them easier to execute because your conscious connection with Holy Spirit will be easier to maintain. You will find, especially as you look back on your journal, that the fears and the feeling of being overwhelmed at the prospect of making the necessary changes in your minds perception of relationships becomes more and more distant, lighter and lighter in emphasis, and increasingly unnecessary to hold onto.

In completion of this step, use the following guidelines:

- The conscious choice for my mind's salvation daily.
- Identification of possible conflictual interactions in which I choose to see Heaven instead of my ego thoughts.
- Journal entries in which I dialogue with the Holy Spirit on lessons of love's awakening.
- I notice increasing ease and peace of mind, as I look with curious anticipation rather, than fearful and worrisome expectation at the unfolding of relationships.

A precious truth arrives and is born within us.

Within our emptiness.
We accept it, we observe it, we absorb it.
We surrender to our bare truth.
We are nourished, we are changed.
We are blessed. We rise up.
For this we give thanks.
Amen.
-Michael Leunig from A Common Prayer

Chapter 7

Claiming Our Mind's Creation

Deep peace of the running wave to you
Deep peace of the flowing air to you
Deep peace of the quiet earth to you
Deep peace of the shining stars to you
Deep peace of the gentle night to you
Moon and stars pour their healing light on you
Deep peace to you
-Shaina Noll

For many years we have learned that the world is only what can be seen or touched by our physical senses. We now come to find out that the Real World is the world of Heaven on Earth in that all things that we perceive with our body's senses are really just physical manifestations of our relationship with ourselves, with God, and with our fellow human beings.

During the course of walking this spiritual path, we take each step closer to embracing our relearning about the nature of our One and Universal Mind's Creation, of which we are an integral part. Our reawakening to the World of Creation, which can also be thought of as Heaven on Earth, is nothing less than a return to sanity through a discipline of mind correction. As we begin to replace our ego thought habits with thoughts of forgiveness and the attention to miracles, we find that more and more of our judgment and attachment to physical objects, as well as our dependence upon what we believe is our image and identity in our social context, begin to fall away. This is analogous to the melting of icicles into their fluid form—water. The substance remains the same, but when allowed to expand, there is a greater flow of our mind's thoughts, of our willingness to reach out in love, in peace, and with an open heart to our fellow human beings.

In practical terms, Creation is every opportunity that we have to exercise miracles on a transpersonal level. When we say transpersonal, we mean heart-to-heart. We have already practiced diligently how we can save our mind through the active expression of miracles toward others. If we add the concept of our joining in Truth with our fellow human beings within the eternal grace of God, then we have the framework for all Creation. Imagine that we are all little drops of water, each with its own place in the ocean, and yet each with its own purpose to interface with the other drops. If we were not able to be in our place in the ocean, there would be an empty spot. Although we have a small identity in our one little drop (our individual mind), we are interconnected with all the other drops that make the huge ocean (the universe.)

Let's go back for a moment to our previous analogy of water in the form of ice. A piece of ice cannot truly intermix with water surrounding it until that ice melts. And so it is, that in Creation we must set aside any barriers, any blocks that we may be tempted to use to judge another as different than and separate from ourselves. We acknowledge the Creator in our mind using the awareness of miracles, forgiveness of illusory transgressions, and willingness to call upon the Holy Spirit. We blend and mingle as our hardheaded thinking melts into the drops of a flowing stream leading to a momentary pool of rest. In each of our thought choices, we choose to see our similarities, our Oneness. This is our true salvation.

Our loving state of mind was never lost, it is simply being re-established. And so, our release to consciously live through eyes that see the Kingdom of Heaven on earth becomes all that we want. Through our willingness, we shall have it. Our conscious union with the Holy Spirit, the Voice for God strengthens as we sharpen our awareness of miracles and see our fellows with increasing clarity through forgiveness. Each and every moment of our waking day serves as our entrance to re-view the world in a limitless fashion.

We begin to understand that we can only project onto our fellows our image of holiness as we look into our own holy minds. Our projections become increasingly loving in nature as they replace projected judgments. God is invited continuously into our waking consciousness as we see through disciplined meditation and open willingness to live love as our primary frame of mind. We focus with increasing acuity using our spiritual eyes onto what has always been. The holy light of God now shines upon all our focused attention.

Are we afraid of Creation? At times, its brilliance and our release from stress itself provokes the ego thought system to sound the fear alarm. We may have held onto fear for so long, that we have come to believe without vigilance, we will parish in our own naïve bliss. Are we afraid of love itself? Are we like the northern vacationer who is afraid to take his coat off when traveling to warm climates out of fear that if he does, he will be that much more shocked when back in the cold? Many of us, deep down inside, do not feel that we deserve to be loved, let alone convey it to others.

Yet, as we open ourselves to miracles, we realize there is no reason to be afraid of love for it is both endless and beyond any need to ask. All you need do is welcome and enjoy. The world awaits our glad acceptance, our openness to love, our free expression of good will, joy and eternal friendship, which helps free others who in part still feel bound by their fears, whether recognized or not. To awaken ourselves is to help awaken others.

When we call upon the Voice for God, the Holy Spirit, we open ourselves to an infinite number of God's thoughts in the form of miracles. We see abundant opportunity to change an unloving thought, to correct an unloving perception, and thereby invite others to do the same. Only love is real. We are the Children of God who are entitled to our own becoming, a life filled with miracle opportunities. Beyond our doubts and fears, we know this for certain. We can see this when we feel closeness with other people, when we see the beauty of nature, when we feel compassion for those who appear to be hurting, when our hearts go out to those who are in need.

All of this reminds us of our certainty. We are all joined in one mind, all joined in love. God's memory is in our holy minds, which know unity with Creation. As we walk down this path, we let our function be only to let our remembering return. We allow for God's loving will to be done in Heaven on Earth. We hear God's voice every day as we walk to the altar in our minds and we converse openly with God in the name of Creation. From there, we feel the power of our own holiness.

Buddha, Moses, Jesus of Nazareth, Mohammed, Mother Theresa, Krishnamurti, Ghandhi or any number of others have shown themselves to be open vessels of the Voice for God. Their examples inspire us to lift ourselves beyond any titles, any exterior roles that we assume, beyond any identity we derived in physical doings. We take every moment of opportunity to exercise a heartfelt being with ourselves, with our fellow human beings, by calling upon the everlasting presence of God.

To call upon universal consciousness, which we know as God, we must be willing to allow our flow of energy to be directed in the most helpful way we can. We come to look beyond the physical aspects of another person and see only the childlike and Godlike qualities within them. This may be through words, gestures, deeds, or just being present to another.

We sense our own willingness to join with the childlike spirit of our partner as we feel our ease at conversing while looking deeply into their eyes, and by noticing our own ease of breathing. When we feel relaxed, our minds can resonate with theirs. This moment of resonance is Co-creation. And thus, when two or more are gathered in His/Her name, there is One. We lose our small selves, only to rediscover our Universal Minds in God's name. We may then allow ourselves to be truly helpful. We fall into Seva, Sanskrit for devotion to God's service, in the name of love and companionship.

> *The dark thought, the shame, the malice,*
> *Meet them at the door laughing*
> *And invite them in.*
>
> *Be grateful for whoever comes,*
> *Because each has been sent*
> *As a guide from beyond.*
> *-Rumi*

Waking Meditation

Upon completion of your deep breathing meditation, open your mind to any particular person that the Holy Spirit would show to you while in your relaxed state. This person is your teacher, as the Holy Spirit has directed you to look in the mirror of projections that you have placed upon him or her. You may have placed judgment to justify separation in your own mind between you and them, and therefore between you and God. What separations we place in our minds upon one person, we have placed upon a Child of God within and therefore upon all.

We must undo these projections to save our minds and more fully open up to awareness of Creation. Allow yourself to notice errors of judgment that God would show you in these meditations. After completing this morning meditation, make an entry in your pocket notebook of those complaints that your mind has held against this person (who is actually you in common spirit). The meditations below will release you from this ego-oriented self-punishment.

Step 1:

During the course of the day, at least once every several hours, look at your notebook. See the reminder phrases that you have written and as you meet others, ask the Voice for God, the Holy Spirit, to release you from the particular judgment that has kept you from joining with them. Once having taken a few moments to do so, consciously look into the eyes of your fellow and wait to be told what is in common between you and the other person. This can be something rather simple, or something well beyond words.

Consciously make remarks within your conversation about how similar you are in certain ways. Use as many examples as you can comfortably apply. Notice the feeling in your heart and mind. You may be sensing lightness, a release from fear and guilt, breaking of ice, and an ease of communication.

Step 2:

During these same encounters, watch yourself in your listening style. Notice if there are times when you didn't really understand what the other person said and/or the emotional and spiritual message above what was said. Practice listening to the call for love in any conversation which tends to be covered over by an earthly topic. Above each conversation is an interest on every person's part to feel accepted, wanted, appreciated and recognized as a Child of God .

Practice moments when you can hear the call for love, when there is a desire for a kind word, reassurance, humor and heartfelt goodwill being asked for by the other party. If you can identify these moments, set aside the topic under discussion and rise up directly to the relationship topic that you are hearing between the lines. There is no need to hesitate. There is no need to allow fearful thoughts to stand in the way of this divine inspiration. Simply view the encounter from this higher viewpoint. Let your own words come from your mouth as placed there by the Holy Spirit.

Once you have begun to ask the Voice for God, the Holy Spirit to direct your words, you will be surprised. With some practice you will be totally guided in what to say or not to say during those moments. Practice this during each day as often as you can, and you will be able to hear with a sense that you may not have previously thought you possessed . This is an intuitive sense, one that we have never lost. We have just lost faith in it temporarily.

After selected discussions of this nature, jot down in your notebook some of your major impressions of these conversations, and especially the feeling of spiritual connectedness within that conversation. Make a note when you feel the presence of God entering the room and this conversation

Guided Imagery Meditation

Upon completion of your deep breathing meditation, imagine yourself in a comfortable setting, one that is both familiar and peaceful to you. As you continue your deep breathing, allow the natural and familiar setting to infuse within your soul and your spirit. As you look around you, see and feel much space. Invite the Holy Spirit to enter this space. Notice the difference in light and colors which will be shown to you through the Holy Spirit's entry into your mind. Just allow this process to unfold without conjuring it up. The shift in consciousness will become apparent.

Now think of one person with whom you would like to remove the barriers of love between you. Let that person walk into the space and ask the Holy Spirit how you may see this person differently. Let them become surrounded by the light of the Holy Spirit and you will see their physical appearance change in front of you. You will notice a change in their eyes, and in their facial expressions, as your mind becomes infused with the light of the Holy Spirit. Let your heart melt through the guidance of the Voice for God and our willingness. Let that person tell you how they may be of some help to you should you allow yourself to open up to them.

Now bring others into this vision, one at a time, as the Holy Spirit, the Voice for God, directs you. Let them gather in a small circle in front of you and within the light which envelops you and them together. When it is possible for you, let your mind merge with each one of theirs, letting their lessons, strength and commonality merge with your own. See yourselves as the droplets in the ocean, both supporting each other and interacting in a flow which is directed by pure spontaneity.

Infused with this ethereal energy, feel yourself becoming lighter as your physical appearance disappears into the air, and you rise into the sky. Now imagine yourself as a cloud floating above the earth. See the earth moving under you. Feel your weightlessness as you are supported by all of the molecules of air in just the right place at just the right moment.

Now float back down to the earth as a tiny seed, almost insignificant in form. Feel yourself beginning to sprout as your little roots take hold, following a grand plan laid out well before the beginning of time. The elements which come from exactly the right place in exactly the right mix help you expand your many molecules, making a thick stalk, then branches, which sprout more branches and leaves.

As you continue with this process, feel the continual presence of miracles, which happen only through your openness to these events. Feel the everlasting sunlight upon your leaves which help sustain you. Feel the nourishing earth that feeds your roots. We are given all the nutrients we need, to feel joy and faith in God's guidance of our spiritual evolution.

When you are ready to close this guided imagery, let your mind come back to the group of people who were shown to you in the first part of this meditation. They were brought to you to bless you in your own grand plan as you allow them to affect you in just the right way in the name of God's Creation, and without imposing your own expectations. When you have completed the meditation, take your notebook and jot down some impressions.

Journal Entries

Review your entries within the pocket notebook of potential judgments you may hold against certain persons, as described in the meditation above. In the evening, as you dialogue with the Holy Spirit, recall those efforts you made to retrain your perceptions to seeing the commonality between you and these persons. Read over the entries you made as you reflected upon the call for love you were able to hear beneath what the other person was saying. Pick a few of these conversations and dialogue in your journal with the Holy Spirit, who will point out to you the Holy moments when true communication occurred, not just between you and the other person, but between you and your Child of God within.

Let the Holy Spirit use whatever visions from the guided imagery concerning the transformed perceptions of those upon whom you may previously judged or condemned. Let these changing images serve as guidelines for improved awareness of areas for opening your mind's perceptual loving creations. You will find that these images will evolve and deepen each time you do this meditation and fall into the ever-present guidance of the Holy Spirit.

Affirmation to be said and thought as often as you are inspired:

"Dear God, let my mind open to the perfect identity that you would have me see."

When it is time to move on:

·   A greater ease of discernment in the process of spiritual communication with another person while entering the true Kingdom of Heaven that occurs when we open our mind to Creation.

·   An increased intuitive ability in listening to the Holy Spirit, the Voice for God. Recognizing how and when you can be truly helpful and helped in a relationship, which becomes a Holy Encounter.

·   Increasingly remove barriers to love in each encounter with another as we consciously ask the Holy Spirit to release our earthly roles and judgments that keep us thinking we are separate within our small minds.

·   Notice your projections onto others are increasingly positive and bountiful, signaling your mind is increasingly filling with the identification with the Universal Mind, the Mind of Creation.

When you feel that these processes have become more habitual, you are ready to go on to the next step.

Existence will remain meaningless for you
If you do not penetrate into it with active love.
Everything is waiting to be hallowed by you.
Meet the world with the fullness of your being
And you shall meet God.
If you wish to believe, love!
-Martin Buber

Chapter 8

The Real World of Vision

The Bud stands for all things
Even for those things that don't flower,
For everything flowers from within of self blessing;
Though sometimes it is necessary to reteach a thing its
loveliness,
To put a hand on the brow of a flower,
And retell it in words and in touch, it is lovely
Until it flowers again from within of self-blessing.
-Galway Kinnel, from St. Francis and the Sow

At this point in our disciplined spiritual path, we begin to suspect that the state of mind of Heaven on Earth is the Real World, the natural state of mind. We can now see ideas we place in our mind tend to grow, whether they are spiritually based or ego based. We have discovered that peace of mind is what we want. We have known this all our lives and we can achieve peaceful periods of thought by refocusing and recalling who we truly are. We have seen while using specified, prescribed steps, we can alter our perceptions of ourselves, relationships, and events.

However, this state of mind cannot be achieved without the correct beginning. We open ourselves to the Holy Spirit to guide us through our process. There is a comfort in remembering this. Our previous frame of mind was self-centered. Now we take this small leap of faith. If we can remain Self-centered, (capital S refers to seeing through the Holy Spirit's eyes), we will enjoy increased periods of continual grace.

As stated previously, we must expect a miracle in every moment. This step (willingness) we must do strictly on our own. It is our free will. Beyond that first step, the Kingdom of Heaven is ours because we have in truth asked for it. There are no further conditions.

In the last several chapters, we have practiced both asking for and receiving the Holy Spirit's input. Through this input , our peaceful frame of mind develops through forgiveness. Now we are ready to ask for a larger share of our time to be blessed in this state. The Real World is the state of the Kingdom of Heaven on earth. It stands for the opposite of what our ego sees. It is the opposite of the world seen through eyes of fear and trepidation. It is the world in which forgiveness blesses us first.

The witnessing of fearful thoughts and fearful activities is a waste of our precious time because when we concentrate on them we divert ourselves away from our true purpose of shining the light of love upon the world. We have found that what we thought were real discrepancies, conflicts and misunderstandings in relationships are the opposite of the Real World. No matter what seeming differences of opinion we have, we can always approach any relationship with an open mind and belief that the Holy Spirit can show us the real channel of healing, our call for love and appreciation.

Any seeming conflict is an opportunity for learning how we can choose again, away from conflict. When we expect a state of Heaven surrounding us, all sights and sounds are gentle in our minds. The Real World arises through a mind of forgiveness, a mind choosing to deal with peaceful solutions evident within our desires. No real danger lurks in anything forgiveness sees, since all the mind expects is kindness.

Sometimes, however, we are caught off guard. Many of us have been taught to seek the 'power' the ego promises. We have sought to be better than, greater, than, and richer than others. We have been taught this is a key to security and a ticket to keeping us alive. Yet, it buys us only a roller coaster effect. When we race with the ego, enough is never enough because in the ego world, there is always someone bigger, better, and seemingly more powerful and ominous. The roller coaster never stops, is never still. Without stillness, we cannot find peace.

Our alternative is clear. There is no race. As we seek our purpose through the Real World, the world of loving interactions, we will be guided to our vast unified kingdom of Heaven on Earth.

Ego thought habits do not give up easily. The ego may label these thoughts of releasing ourselves from the rat race of victimhood as naïve, as seeing ourselves as reaching for an overly blissful state of mind. When we become frightened by this state, we may jump back into our zealous self-protection. We may even chastise ourselves for taking ourselves off guard. This is partly what keeps us on an emotional roller coaster. When we achieve brief moments of inner peace, the ego cries out 'enough!', almost without fail. Off we go to pay the price the ego would have us pay for inner peace.

The Real World puts no price on the giving and receiving of miracles of love. Love's energy costs nothing and requires no conditions. We need not do or think anything special. We only need to be willing to open up to miracle opportunities in every moment. Would it not be better to maintain an even and faithful outlook and avoid the strain and stressful waste of elusive highs and depressing lows? Too simple? The ego would say yes, and puts us back on the emotional roller coaster.

As our practice of seeking peace deepens, we come to realize that there is no compromise position with the ego. The ego glorifies fear as a necessary way of life. The Holy Spirit knows of no fear. It is insanity to keep trying to balance the two. The two cannot coexist. When our minds get on the ego bus, we get off the free ride of the Holy Spirit.

Our choice can be made in a Holy Instant. If we want peace of mind, we can always choose to fill our minds with loving and compassionate thoughts.

When we fill our mind with our willingness to see the Real World, our attention naturally goes to those miraculous qualities around us, which verify we are surrounded by God's love.

Our bodies are our exquisite communication devices, helping us to glean physical sensations, which our minds and hearts translate into spiritual blessings given unto us. We are grateful for those sensations rather than judge them. The temperature around us becomes neither cold nor hot. Our body's sensations simply attest that we are alive to feel these temperatures. The taste of food represents the care and interest of its preparation. We feel the love in that preparation. And so the miracle in the tasting of food is recognition that we have a body that can taste. The taste reaches up to our eternal state of satisfaction as we gratefully receive offerings of those folks who are willing to lovingly prepare the meal.

Our Real World thinking reaches for the verification of joy in our experiences. The breeze blowing the branches of trees shows us the balance of exquisite nature. They regulate themselves in concert with the totality of the elements, which are always a part of our life giving nourishment. The refreshing smells and fragrances that spread the message that all sensations and elements are part of a total grand plan of which we have an essential part.

The way a bird will seek the air currents allowing it to soar above the ground, seemingly without effort, becomes a lesson in the power of God's glory. We can place ourselves in a position to ride with the current of energy which keeps us above and detached from all that appears to be pressing in our lives. It's from this point of detachment that we are carried up to look at the whole gestalt of all that unfolds. So we see the essential in blessings.

We realize that alas, we can go off into the detour of justifying our need for our ego thought processes. We can point to an infinite number of examples in this world which engender fear. We choose consciously not to go there. We choose rather, not to waste our thoughts on debate. Our emphasis here is to enhance the awareness of the state of Heaven on Earth, the Real World.

Surely, we would all admit that we need more of that process and less fear thoughts in their many forms. Each one of those forms boils down to a fear of separation from God. In the path that we have chosen for our deliberate studies, we are reaffirming our constant alignment with the love of God. We are never alone, and only need to re-mind ourselves through our open spiritual awareness of the Real World.

We cannot fail to feel the eternal working of God in the powers that create oceans from the coalescing of gasses, support a chain of life extending from the tiniest of creatures to the mightiest, in the free choices that are given us, and in the interweaving of each moment of miracles. Yet, God is so gentle as to be the softest voice we will ever hear and yet the truest. God's infinite patience helps us to choose again as we gradually shed our own emotional imprisonment. The more we seek the Real World of the Kingdom of Heaven on earth in our daily training, the faster we release the bonds holding down our free spirit and partake of the abundance of miracles given and received.

> There are two ways of living one's life,
> One is as though nothing is a miracle,
> The other is if everything is a miracle.
> -Albert Einstein

Waking Meditation

Upon completion of the deep breathing meditation, open your mind to seemingly small things that are happening around you. Begin by saying, "This small event has a world of meaning within it." Then take in that small event, letting the Holy Spirit show you the continuity of all events that have led to this one moment in time being brought to your attention.

Pick one such event such as an ant crawling on the table. Let your mind be shown that the ant is responding to its part in a grand plan of where it is to go while crawling upon a table. The table, which came from a place from which it was manufactured, which came from where the wood was harvested and milled, which came from where the tree was grown, which was nourished, perhaps, in part by the death of a small insect such as an ant, indicating an eternal unfolding of events in just the right way. The ant crawling on the table in front of you shows you a blessing, the blessing of the continuity of life. The blessing carries with it God's continual promise that all unfolds as it should, and is beyond our need for understanding.

As another example we may focus our attention on the swinging of branches of a tree in the breeze. The wind of the breeze gathers up at just the right moment to affect the branches and then passes on while allowing the tree to correct its posture. The tree becomes stronger each time it is given this interaction with the elements. Your attention to this branch swaying in the breeze is a gift given to yourself and allows you to be reminded of other lessons of the Real World. It may indicate to you all things pass as we remain flexible.

As another example, you may hear the singing of a particular bird in the distance, and that particular pitch reverberates in your heart. Suddenly we allow ourselves to feel a vast connectedness spreading across the land and through our minds unabashedly. The examples in even a few moments of awareness can be endless. We feel the collage of personal and particular miracles being shown to us to affirm the presence of the Kingdom of Heaven, the Real World as we tune in around us and within us.

Here is another helpful example that illustrates the multitude of effects of this waking exercise. When we see these letters: NOWHERE, we can read them out of habit from a sleeping mind or we can choose to awaken to the message the Holy Spirit would have us see. Physically, they are only letters on this page. Will you put the effort in to ask yourself what you are to see? When you do, what will you be shown? You could see NOWHERE, NO WHERE, or NOW HERE. No matter what answer you have received, the search itself is what the Real World is about and what brings you to your truthful answers.

Short waking meditation

This is simply to emphasize that any tiny moment using the above concentrated focus can be every bit as powerful as longer meditations. The spiritual message contained in these moments of awareness come to you instantaneously without any analysis. If you have a few extra moments, jot down these awarenesses in your notebook.

Guided Imagery Meditation

Upon completion of your deep breathing meditation, see a majestic eagle sitting in front of you in your mind's eye. See its wide wingspan and profuse array of feathers as they lie smoothly and perfectly over its entire body. Look into the eagle's keen eyes and the majesty of its head sitting boldly upon its commanding torso. After becoming completely immersed in this vision, let yourself melt into the eagle. Feel the power and the courage of the character of this mighty spirit. Let yourself jump off your perch into the trade winds, which carry you in your soaring. As you look down, see all of the beauty, wonder and interweaving tapestry of the landscape elements below you.

Now ask the Holy Spirit to show you a particular landscape, and then a particular part of the landscape. Allow the Holy Spirit to guide you to either rise to see a larger picture or to glide downward to see a close up of particular views. Notice what is being shown to you in this tour. Is the search for beauty, for serenity in seeing the interconnectedness of all things, for food, or for other spiritual or emotional nourishment?

As you place yourself in the arms of the Voice for God, the Holy Spirit, is showing you a journey of personal discovery. Each time you take flight in the winds, what you see and experience becomes a fascinating surprise. You are shown what you are ready to see. Notice the effect on your mind and body when you listen truly, as you meditatively soar on the wings of the Holy Spirit, buoyed by God's eternal energy.

As you are soaring, call for a distant memory of when you flew in this area at a much younger age. Let yourself be shown how your perceptions have changed and what wisdom you have acquired in these travels. Recognize familiar animals with whom you have previously had any encounters. Greet them and bless them, whether or not they are aware of your presence above. Notice the effects upon your mind and upon what you see in them when you bless them. See how the landscape has changed and notice the benefits those changes have brought to the inhabitants below and to yourself. Bless yourself for being able to see this transformation toward peace as you soar with the wings of Heaven. Make note of the miracles shown to you upon ending this meditation.

Journal Entries

As you reflect on your pocket notebook entries from the waking meditations, and you will find a very active dialogue with the Voice for God, the Holy Spirit. Your frame of mind in seeing every day events somehow more reverently as continuity of our Real World of love becomes easier to discern.

As you review your notes of miracles shown you through your guided imagery meditation, allow yourself to dialogue with the Holy Spirit, the Voice for God on the topic of being willing to see and appreciate readily the Kingdom of Heaven on earth.

Affirmation to be said and thought as often as you are inspired:

"My perception of the Real World of the Kingdom of Heaven on earth arises from my mind, seeking peace with itself."

When it is time to move on:

Practice the above meditations for as long as you feel you need. We can now begin to intersperse them with the previous meditations we used in earlier chapters based on your personal decision and guided through your inspiration with the Holy Spirit, the Voice for God.

Please try to complete, in part, the following tasks before going on to the next step.

· An increasing sense of peace, regardless of exter-

nal circumstances as we rely more on our conscious awareness of the Real World, The Kingdom of Heaven on earth.

· Willingness and continual practice of seeing God's
blessings in seemingly small events surrounding you.

· The expectation of continual miracles and our
willingness to attend to these miracles.

· Increasing comfort in guided imagery showing
you the blessings of our evolving purpose of illuminating
love as inspired through the Holy Spirit, the Voice for God.

The shifting scenes of life screen the true Life:
Behind the unreal motion pictures of things seen
Unfolds the real drama of Stable cosmic life unseen.

This world is but a stage in which you play your parts
Under the direction of the Divine Stage Manager.

Play them well, whether they are tragic
Or comic, always remembering
That your real nature is eternal Bliss.
-Paramahansa Yogananda

Chapter 9

Recognizing The Child of God Within

Our potential to love is very real
And is somehow not destroyed,
No matter what we experience;
All of the mistakes we make,
All the times that we are caught in reaction,
All of the times that we have caused pain,
All of the times we have suffered.
Troughout everything, our potential to love
Remains intact and pure.

-Sharon Salzberg, from Loving Kindness
The Revolutionary Art of Happiness

We now become ready to invite all relationships to enter our holy state of mind where God resides. Now, we are concentrating on taking a stand to see the holiness in others as the seat of our own salvation. Again, this may not be easy, since we all have the continual habit of judging others, an unfortunate justification of our differences Let us place in our minds thoughts of greatest intention to see beneath judgments. Our goal is to see only the childlike qualities underneath the rhetoric and outside appearances of others. We now open the door to welcome that part of our minds that can only see the request for loving attention on the part of our fellow travelers in this world. As we do so, we call upon the Holy Spirit to show us our perfect selves as well.

Our Child of God within is as simple and innocent as a newborn baby. There are no grudges, no illusion of despair, no left over anger. The Child of God within, our spiritual essence, resides in a place of knowing, our symbolic altar. The Child of God within is always willing to seek and receive loving kindness right now. Beyond the ego reticence, we invite this part of ourselves into our awareness daily. We invite our Child of God within to go beyond preoccupations and self-conscious attachments of the way we look, the way we sound, and the way we dress. We see these melting away before our very eyes. It is in this simple and innocent context that the Voice for God, the Holy Spirit, can reach within us to give the simple answers to life's mysteries.

Through One-minded intention, thoughts of anger, and struggle previously perceived to be so real merely slip away from our interest, and even from our consciousness. We find it much easier to place a framework of forgiveness upon the world, and to see only requests for peace from *every* Child of God within. As we see the Child of God within each other, we begin to see our mind gravitating beyond past overlays, future insecurities, and focusing itself only on the current request for love. As we behold the glory of our fellow human being, as we see the Child within, we remember how learning becomes a very simple task. The only question involved is 'how might I be of help?' or put another way, 'how might I be a teacher of love in this particular moment?'

The Child of God within is guiltless. All intentions have ultimately led us to exactly where we are today. At no time has God ever withheld everlasting and complete acceptance and unconditional regard even as we believed we were walking a path of suffering. God's faith in us is our model. Our faith in ourselves is what creates faith in others. That faith is undying. When we are tempted to berate ourselves for some perceived past wrong-doing or omission, we only need to remember the unqualified love which God has for us, and we will be reminded of our innocence. Recognizing our own guiltlessness, we approach our fellow human beings in a like -minded manner, seeing them guiltless as well. Our minds' surrender to peace becomes a total belief in spiritual lessons flowing from seeming errors. The ultimate lesson is always recognizing where our home is and where our greatest resource for companionship lies.

Simplicity itself sets the stage for us to allow the joy of the Child of God within to arise. In simplicity, we need not protect ourselves from what comes before us on life's path. As we take a moment extra to tap into that place of knowing, our Child of God within can look upon each event as an opportunity that leads only to the next, and therefore eventually down a path which is always in our own best interest. Our path is filled with the greatest abundance, given us simply for the asking. Each step fully taken in this light fills us with the love of God.

Our Child of God within can be easily ignored through the ego's idolatry. We can cloud the bright star of the Child of God within through our own self-limiting thoughts of separation based on seemingly physical differences and through fear of death in its many forms. Therefore, we ask to continuously converse with the Child of God within.

Our triad team of spiritual communication leading to our own salvation is: God, the Holy Spirit, and the Child of God. We become fully aware that the Voice for God, the Holy Spirit, which we experience to be our intuitive guidance and direction, only speaks in simple terms, most readily understood by the Child of God within. We invite the Child of God within into our awareness, as we consciously simplify our thoughts so that they may be expressions of pure love.

At first we use the simplest of words, and later we search beneath words. Once we place the Child of God within the center of all communication with each other, our encounter becomes a holy one. As time goes on, we see only the face of innocence, the face of friendship, the face of love in each person we see and hear. Each face that we see shows us the way in which we can communicate love with that integral and sacred part of our Selves (God).

It is through our dialogue with the Child of God within that forgiveness becomes a natural frame of mind in relating to each other and towards our selves. We unblock our minds from its' only purpose, the illumination of God's love. As we tune into the Child of God within, we shine away from ego thoughts that would hamper us with fear's illusions. Instead, we see readily through the Child of God within opportunities for joining, relating, and truly empathizing.

The Child of God within sees only the commonality within our souls. We see, through consistent meditative practice, our feelings of endearment to ourselves and others intensify. The Child of God within shows us the World of Heaven, a place where there is no separation between us. As we tap into the Child of God within, we come to that place of knowing that only the thoughts of shared joy have meaning.

> God, I offer myself to you
> To build with me and do with me what You will.
> Relieve me of the bondage of myself
> That I may better do your will.
> May I do your will always.
> -From the Big Book of Alcoholics Anonymous
> (adapted)

Waking Meditation

Upon completion of our morning deep breathing meditation, ask the Holy Spirit, the Voice for God, for an opportunity to practice giving miracles of unconditional love and affection. As we give, we receive, so of course this is an exercise in self-love as well.

To begin, let yourself manifest a project, object or living creature and/or activity that you choose to hold in your affection and love. The object of our affection may be a plant, a hobby, a form of service rendered, or a pet, among others. Ideally, this focus should inspire you to use as many of your senses as possible, including the senses of smell and touch.

One example that comes to mind is a young kitten. As you give yourself several minutes to bestow unconditional affection upon the kitten, you will merge with its kindred spirit. Look deeply into its eyes and pet it. Feel an exchange of comfort and love, which you are able to convey back and forth to each other. Sense the slowing of the animal's heartbeat as it relaxes and lets itself fall into your embrace. Loose yourself in the interchange.

As you do so, you will find that you will take great pleasure in giving pleasure. As you impart loving affection to this animal you may notice, all other things in your mind fade away. In your moments of giving, you will find that the world feels increasingly simple. This is the experience of the Child of God within, the pure and simple joy of being.

In the next step of this waking meditation, place yourself in the position of receiver, within your mind's eye. All gifts given are also given to ourselves. Let's continue to use the example of the kitten. As you continue to stroke your pet, lose your separate self and actually become the kitten, the object of your affection. Let yourself receive your own gifts. Feel worthy of your own perfection.

Notice the shift in your mind, lightness in thought, and an ease in which joy rises within your spirit. Notice how right receiving love feels. Let your heart sink into the heart of love. Let your mind fully accept your loving glory as a Child of God. Let your mind awaken to the love which is forever present for us from our Father/Mother/God. We only need remember these peaceful and joyful moments of love's presence for our mind's expansiveness to grow.

And when you feel ready to face the day, take with you a piece of these emotions. Let them stay in the forefront of your mind, regardless of other thoughts, physical pain, or other forms of upset that your ego would bring to your attention. You will notice these other discomforts will not totally disappear from your awareness, yet will reduce in significance.

Short Waking Meditation

During the course of the day, whenever you come across an upsetting event, relive that moment in your mind and then step back. Choose for the love of God, unconditionally, and actively converse about this event with the Holy Spirit and with the Child of God within. The issues involved will simplify considerably into one overall decision. Do we concentrate on a call for love or on a call for fear interpretation.

Envision the faces of those who are involved. See them as little children. Superimpose upon them the face of the Child of God within. Ask only, "in what form are they calling for my love?" Notice any shift in your thinking and outlook on this matter. Jot these occurrences down in your notebook, and in the evening, reflect on them as you dialogue with the Voice for God, the Holy Spirit.

Guided Imagery Meditation

Upon completion of your daily deep breathing meditation, in your mind's eye, approach your altar and see laid upon it a young infant wrapped in the simplest of comfortable blankets. Look deeply into the child's face. See all the details of that face. Look deeply into the child's eyes. That child is yourself, not only the child that you were, but that you still are. Pick up the child and hold the child as you continue to look deep into its soul. See the slightest nuances of mannerisms and expressions the child will show you. Feel the child's heartbeat inside of you.

And now, let yourself ask this child a mature adult-like complicated question that is bothering you. Notice, the child will understand the question only as an infant would. The child will reduce that question to the very basic one of whether it senses from you love or fear. Let yourself feel the simple joy and humor in this encounter, and allow yourself to pare down that question. Bring it down to its greatest simplicity. Then ask yourself, do I wish to approach this question out of fear, or out of love? Upon opening your eyes, jot down a few words about the comparison which you have recognized between the responses of your ego-centered mind and of that part of your mind which is the Child of God.

In the evening, reflect back on your notebook phrases as you dialogue with the Holy Spirit. Let yourself be shown again, the endless wisdom of simplicity. Allow yourself to apply these lessons in your waking life wherever you find they are useful to you. Continue to keep an open dialogue with the Child of God within, who is most able to hear the Voice for God, the Holy Spirit.

Journal Entries

Write down your very active involvement as you exchange moments of loving as in our first meditation above. Let the Holy Spirit encourage your discovery as a Child of God.

Review your entries on how you were able to capture moments

during the day to teach love. Describe the faces of the 'children' calling for love during your day. Use your guided imagery meditation to reduce seemingly complicated involvements into their most basic simplifications. Write down examples and dialogue with the Holy Spirit.

Each moment that we translate a seeming misunderstanding or challenge into a lesson of love, we sense in our minds a greater opening to focus on our ability to teach love. We have then walked another step towards our own freedom. To teach love, be love.

Affirmation to be said and thought as often as you are inspired:

> *"I will place the Child of God upon the altar within my mind."*

When it is time to move on:

Continue with these daily meditations along with those of our previous steps as you are directed. Feel increasing peace as you:

- Recognize the ongoing dialogue of love, appreciation and affection between the Voice for God and the Child of God within.
- Pare down concerns that approach you in your mind. Shift into the basic question of how we may help to spread and illuminate love unconditionally.
- Through meditation, allow yourself to see the Child of God in others, as continual expression of love's perfection.
- Notice the intensity of attachments to what the

ego would have us worry about, and use to cloud our minds from thoughts of love. Choose to listen to the Child of God instead.

Hold us in your embrace, Lord
Make us transparent in your light.
Grant us your awareness;
Keep our gratitude fresh each day.
Let our song give blessing and insight
To those who can't see for themselves.
And let your compassion always shine forth
From the depths of our hearts.
-from Psalm 40, rendered by Stephen Mitchell

Chapter 10

I Am

The phrase "I am" has been used in many contexts to summarize the ultimate choice in our existence. We choose to be the totality of our spiritual being, open and ready to be a servant and teacher of God. In the past, we may have answered the question posed by another person of "who are you?" in terms of the roles we play in our daily existence. We may have answered with our occupation, with our family status, with our financial status or with our attachments to objects. We may have answered with a label we placed upon physical attributes of ourselves. We may have automatically answered with a physical or an emotional feeling state such as "I am happy, angry, depressed," etc. All of these become delimiting thoughts of separation because they exclude the totality of who we are.

The wisdom of Krishnamurti speaks of this totality and a need for a much more deliberate intention in defining who we are.

"When you call yourself an Indian or a Muslim or a Christian or a European, or anything else, you are being violent. Do you see why it is violent? Because you are separating yourself from the rest of mankind. When you separate yourself by belief, by nationality, by tradition, it breeds violence. So a man who is trying to understand violence does

not belong to any country, to any religion, to any political party or partial system; he is concerned with the total understanding of mankind."

We are all and everything–perfect in our imperfection, whole in our potential. We are that unique portion of God we call ourself, yet interconnected with an infinite number of unique parts that are at our disposal, simply by inviting God's conscious presence within our minds. We have found through deliberate practice of our decisions to call upon the Voice for God, that we are helped in directing our thoughts and our perceptions to light up our experience of the world. We are increasingly open to receive miracles great and small and to give of these miracles, which are ours to create. The flow of loving energy passes through us and illuminates from us. We are learning to experience our loving totality by placing aside judgments of separation and differences through the practice of forgiveness. As we forgive, we offer ourselves our own salvation, consciously joining our little selves with our Greater Self in the Universal Mind of God.

So, as we grow into greater awareness, how do we discern who we are? In any given moment in time, we are all that we could ever become. We are the flowing energy of miracles and we are the ministerial witnesses to loving energy in miracles. We are teachers, speaking of God and carrying God's words to everyone who has been sent to us. And yet we need not know what special words to say, what particular activities to perform. In being, we are simply open to what God has in store for us.

How have we placed imagined limits on our unlimited being? This is what our conscious spiritual study has brought to the surface. Now we place our ego thoughts upon our altar daily. We see them vanish simply by seeing them as being false projections. We commit ourselves to experiencing our own joy and happiness daily. We turn in our thoughts of power, control, self-protection and the need to be "right" and exchange them for pleasurable anticipation of what is to come, gratitude for everything that has been experienced, and joy in all present moments.

By now, we have experienced increasing peace and serenity. We are ones who are coming to a heightened awareness of the choices available to us, and we are ones who are remembering what we truly desire from moment to moment. We are realizing that no matter what we end up doing, no matter what role we play in the dance of life, every form of doing that we choose is a matter of being. We literally succeed at any interaction in business, politics, family, or otherwise where we have been the messenger of loving affirmation to the best of our ability. When we fall short, we are not ones who chastise ourselves. We realize that it is part of our spiritual learning process allowing us to be that much more loving in our next encounter of that nature.

Truly committed to our state of a loving mind, there is literally no goal that we can set for ourselves that cannot be accomplished, no amount of success that cannot be reached, no day in which fatigue overtakes us. We have no desire for addictions, no false Gods or idols, no desire to avoid our true reality. Our minds are open, clear, conscious and with a ready confidence that we have the power of prayer and thought which shows us the solutions to all our temporary challenges. We remember again that all questions posed to us lead to an answer which is only for our good and well-being. We claim the courage to face these challenges as they present themselves, knowing we are God's children, and we are blessed with eternal peace.

Who am I? The letter 'I' is a fascinating symbol and a wonderful spiritual symbol. It has a top, and a bottom, and a large pillar in the center. The bottom line is the foundation we stand on, the Earth, and the top line represents Heaven. These parallel lines at the top and bottom could be imagined to reach into infinity. The center post of the pronoun "I" meets at a 90-degree angle both at the bottom and the top. The connectness, which flows in both directions, comes through us, our own spirit. The concept of "I" becomes a symbol of our recognition of our connection between our earthly tasks and the greater meaning of those tasks in the context of Heaven. This makes it stable and solid, held up eternally.

In contrast, the small "i' consists of a single line with a disconnected dot floating above it. Metaphorically, it represents our conscious choice of identity between the Child of God within ('I') and the ego ('i'). As part of our spiritual statement of who we truly are, we choose for 'I'. The pronoun 'I', therefore, is a commitment to place our perception of Heaven, the Real World within all of our earthly experiences. This is exactly what our meditations in this book have been teaching us to become; who I really am.

> You can see the message very clearly,
> Everywhere you look on all sides.
> It comes from the knowers of the Truth of all traditions.
> They all say the same thing:
> Experience God's vastness within yourself,
> But also feed the hungry.
> Experience God's bounty within yourself;
> Also listen to the words of your sorrowful friend.
> Experience God's love in your own being;
> Also don't mind making your own bed
> When you wake up in the morning.
> Both mundane and spiritual belong to God,
> So learn to share with others
> The greatness you experience within yourself.
> -Swami Chidvilasananda (Gurumayi)

Waking Meditation

This meditation can be used as a means of culmination of all the

meditations we have practiced over this period of time. Upon completion of your deep breathing meditation, bring to your physical altar or
in your mind's eye, a particular circumstance in which you have questions about who you are and how you might be a messenger of love.

Review the "Steps Toward Peaceful Solutions" below. After read-
ing through this list, write down after each step whatever guided message is brought to you in response to the circumstance you have brought
to your altar. We need not give this undue contemplation. Answers will
come, as we are ready for them. We can leave some areas blank for
now, if that is most comfortable.

Steps Toward Peaceful Solutions

*I open my mind and heart concerning this matter to the Voice for
God, the Holy Spirit. I wish to set aside the following thoughts which
are fear-based, that keep me from receiving clear messages, which would
guide me.*

*I look to see miracle moments which show me in metaphor and
through my senses, corrective ways of looking at my fear thoughts and
preoccupation with those thoughts. I have seen the following miracles
today.*

*I have been guided to give unconditionally the following miracles,
which are pure expressions of love's energy I have received through
miracles shown me.*

*I have chosen to look differently, beyond judgments on this matter.
I ask only that the Holy Spirit show me the way to see more clearly. I
now write down examples.*

I pay attention to the relief that I feel in my mind as a result of my conscious choices. I bless myself for the relief I am given as part of my own salvation on this matter. Here are thoughts that have come to me.

I open my mind consciously to a general expectation of only a loving outcome. I recognize that every step of the way, the Voice for God will speak through my Child of God within to champion a loving and simple solution. Here are possible outcomes.

These peaceful thoughts of a loving Creation come to me.

I request to be reminded to step back whenever I feel moments of discomfort, breathe deeply, reconnect with the Voice for God, and have faith that I may see this whole context with the eyes of love. Here is how I may see it.

I ask for clarity on this matter by listening to the simple expressions of the Child of God within. Let me be shown and jot down here ways in which I can see and respond only to the request for love. May I learn through the Holy Spirit how I may respond to the call for love with only loving compassion. May I feel as connected with these persons as a drop of water with the ocean. Here are some loving perceptions and responses.

In the evening, review your sheet and dialogue with the Holy Spirit. Where you sense a need for greater release from blocks to love, ask to be shown more clearly love's miraculous transformations in your next day's travels.

Guided Imagery Meditation

Upon completion of your deep breathing meditation, simply envision yourself printing, deliberately and consciously, the words "I AM" in capital letters. Feel yourself holding the writing instrument in your mind, placing it onto the paper with the pressure you select, and writing out the letters. Notice how fast or how slow you go in this writing.

Experiment with being guided in your mind to write the words using different patterns of pressure, style and emphasis on particular parts of the letters. Notice as you try these different patterns in your mind, changes in how you feel. Now, mentally put the pencil aside and look at the words you just wrote. Feel each phrase. Feel the spiritual connectedness of the power of each phrase and each letter within each phrase and each stroke within each letter. Finally, allow your mind to complete the phrase "I am…" with an inspiration you hear/see/feel from the Voice for God. Don't judge its' completion. Merely take it in and let it be. Know with ever increasing clarity that only love is real, and therefore only love is who I am.

Journal Entries

Reflect upon your answers to the 'Steps Towards Peaceful Solutions' above in situations where you are seeking your role as helper and guide to loving and peaceful affirmation. Glean from your answers which meditations in the previous chapters can use some revisiting for further deepening effects.

The 'I AM' excersize above can be done with or without actually writing. If you do the excersize by writing in your journal, notice the minute details of speed and pressure that you apply at various parts of the writing. Deliberately repeat these methods of writing or even exaggerate them. Dialogue with the Holy Spirit on what lessons of love these writing methods may have for you. Also, practice the affirmation below as often as you like.

Affirmation to be said and thought as often as you are inspired:

'I AM'…..Then wait for the answer.

You are me and I am you.
Isn't it obvious that we inter/are?
You cultivate the flower in yourself so I will be beautiful.
I transform the garbage in myself so that you will not
have to suffer.
I support you. You support me.
I am in this world to offer you peace.
You are in this world to bring me joy.
-Thich Nhat Hanh

Epilogue

Congratulate and bless yourself for the courage and committed effort you have given over this period of time in walking this very personal path with the Voice for God to help you recall who you really are and how you can be a more effective instrument of God's love. As we stated earlier, it takes quite a bit of self discipline to continue on with this process. Yet as it becomes more engrained in your thinking, you find that God's presence in helping you to see the world differently, and your willingness in conveying the miracle of bringing a loving presence to others becomes a much more natural way of being. Hopefully your thoughts are clear, your heart lighter, your affect more joyful and your anticipation greater for what your daily blessings may show you.

At this time, please take the Peace Quotient Survey again. Compare the results with the first time that you took it to see where you have made improvements in the process of claiming your own peace of mind. Feel free to continue to use the exercises in this book as you continue to grow on your spiritual life's journey.

Thank you for allowing us to join with you in this effort. If you wish further dialogue, we can be reached at the following addresses and phone numbers:

Scott Anstadt and Deb Byster
4499 Sunrise Lane
Traverse City, MI 49684
www.thesunrisecenter.com or
deb@northlink.net
(231) 929-7023

Peace Quotient Survey

Answer each item subjectively from 1 to 7, with 1 being "I totally disagree" and 7 being "I identify completely with the thought."

·   I seek the voice of the Holy Spirit daily through prayer to help employ the means to restore my mind to where it is truly at home.

(Disagree) 1 2 3 4 5 6 7 (Identify)

·   The Holy Spirit calls to me to let forgiveness rest upon my fearful dreams and restore them to sanity and peace of mind.

(Disagree) 1 2 3 4 5 6 7 (Identify)

·   The Holy Spirit is God's gift, by which the quietness of Heaven is restored to me.

(Disagree) 1 2 3 4 5 6 7 (Identify)

·   A miracle allows for the awakeing of love.

(Disagree) 1 2 3 4 5 6 7 (Identify)

- A miracle is a gift of grace, when giving it, we receive it.

(Disagree) 1 2 3 4 5 6 7 (Identify)

- To see a miracle for what it is brings witness to the fact that God exists.

(Disagree) 1 2 3 4 5 6 7 (Identify)

- Miracles happen all the time. When we don't see them, it's because we have blocked love's presence.

(Disagree) 1 2 3 4 5 6 7 (Identify)

- To ask for a miracle implies that my mind is ready to witness it.

(Disagree) 1 2 3 4 5 6 7 (Identify)

- In his love, God shows me that I am guiltless and I am united with all creation in that love.

(Disagree) 1 2 3 4 5 6 7 (Identify)

- I believe that when I seek the Holy Spirit that thoughts of separation can be replaced with thoughts of peace.

(Disagree) 1 2 3 4 5 6 7 (Identify)

- Salvation means letting go of illusions of differences separating us from each other and from our One Spirit.

(Disagree) 1 2 3 4 5 6 7 (Identify)

·   My salvation rests in radiating the light of God to the world.

(Disagree) 1 2 3 4 5 6 7 (Identify)

·   As I forgive others of what sins I am tempted to see, all my sins are forgiven.

(Disagree) 1 2 3 4 5 6 7 (Identify)

·   Through forgiveness I end the cycle of masking the truth of my fellow being's Godliness

(Disagree) 1 2 3 4 5 6 7 (Identify)

·   To forgive, I only need to ask the Holy Spirit to show me how, and step aside as it is done.

(Disagree) 1 2 3 4 5 6 7 (Identify)

·   A sin is not a call for punishment, it is a choice with consequences which can be painful yet part of my spiritual learning.

(Disagree) 1 2 3 4 5 6 7 (Identify)

·   What God creates is like God.

(Disagree) 1 2 3 4 5 6 7 (Identify)

·   I am creation, a child of God.

(Disagree) 1 2 3 4 5 6 7 (Identify)

- Creation is eternal unity with God.

(Disagree) 1 2 3 4 5 6 7 (Identify)

- Creation is the composite of all of God's thoughts, of loving infinity, which can be seen everywhere when we open our minds.

(Disagree) 1 2 3 4 5 6 7 (Identify)

- My body can be used to heal my mind.

(Disagree) 1 2 3 4 5 6 7 (Identify)

- I use my body to extend my hand to my brother as we walk along the road together.

(Disagree) 1 2 3 4 5 6 7 (Identify)

- I can only see the Real World through forgiving eyes, and a mind at peace.

(Disagree) 1 2 3 4 5 6 7 (Identify)

- When I have forgiven myself, I see only happy sights and sounds.

(Disagree) 1 2 3 4 5 6 7 (Identify)

- The real world is the symbol of my awakening.

(Disagree) 1 2 3 4 5 6 7 (Identify)

· The world I had often seen, one based on fear, is being replaced with a world based on love's visions.

(Disagree) 1 2 3 4 5 6 7 (Identify)

· I increasingly recognize that a world without love is a world without God.

(Disagree) 1 2 3 4 5 6 7 (Identify)

· When my mind is filled with truth, fear can't be present.

(Disagree) 1 2 3 4 5 6 7 (Identify)

· When I seek beyond the chains of fearful thought, I witness the truth of love's perception.

(Disagree) 1 2 3 4 5 6 7 (Identify)

· The release of my belief in fear opens my mind to eternal life.

(Disagree) 1 2 3 4 5 6 7 (Identify)

· A child of God is the Self I share with another and with God as well.

(Disagree) 1 2 3 4 5 6 7 (Identify)

· My child within remains untouched by anything the eyes observe, and remains untouched by thoughts of sin.

(Disagree) 1 2 3 4 5 6 7 (Identify)

· The Holy Spirit reaches from the child within me to all my misperceptions, correcting my thoughts.

(Disagree) 1 2 3 4 5 6 7 (Identify)

· I wish to find the Godliness in my brother's face and nothing else.

(Disagree) 1 2 3 4 5 6 7 (Identify)

· No matter what form my body takes, it is not a barrier to my loving expression.

(Disagree) 1 2 3 4 5 6 7 (Identify)

· I no longer give my body the power to override the spirit that is my true identity.

(Disagree) 1 2 3 4 5 6 7 (Identify)

· God's being resides in me.

(Disagree) 1 2 3 4 5 6 7 (Identify)

· I am a reflection of God's love.

(Disagree) 1 2 3 4 5 6 7 (Identify)

· I exemplify the word of God.

(Disagree) 1 2 3 4 5 6 7 (Identify)

· I am willing to fulfill God's role for me.

(Disagree) 1 2 3 4 5 6 7 (Identify)

- I can choose to see only the goodness in others.

(Disagree) 1 2 3 4 5 6 7 (Identify)

- I can choose to see the goodness in events as they unfold.

(Disagree) 1 2 3 4 5 6 7 (Identify)